The Mystical Message
of the Saints

They are the men and women whose lives of holy dedication to God have lifted them above the mortal realms into the Kingdom of Heaven. Each, through their individual character and by virtue of their words and deeds, exemplifies a particular, unique channel between the earthly and the Divine worlds. Whether their stories are historical, mythic, or allegorical, they inspire us with their spiritual purity and heroism.

With the passage of the centuries the saints have become icons, both literally and figuratively. As living symbols, they are very well suited to manifest through one of the world's most venerated paths to inner understanding and guidance—the Tarot. With this book and the accompanying deck, you will form a much closer relationship with these venerable beings, and benefit directly from their lessons.

From historical insights into the origins of Christianity to the immediacy of answers for the present moment, *A Gnostic Book of Saints* will take you on a journey of enlightenment and spiritual discovery.

About the Author

Robert M. Place is an internationally known visionary artist and illustrator. He is recognized as an expert on the Western mystical tradition and the history and philosophy of the Tarot, and his work has appeared in many books and publications. Place is also the designer, illustrator, and coauthor of the highly acclaimed *Alchemical Tarot* and *The Angels Tarot*. He has appeared on the Discovery Channel and the Learning Channel and has conducted lectures and workshops throughout the country, including the Open Center and the Omega Institute in New York and the International Tarot Congress in Chicago. Place's work in precious metals have been displayed in museums such as the New York State Museum, the American Craft Museum, and the White House.

To Write to the Author

If you wish to contact the author or would like more information about this book, please write to the author in care of Llewellyn Worldwide and we will forward your request. Both the author and publisher appreciate hearing from you and learning of your enjoyment of this book and how it has helped you. Llewellyn Worldwide cannot guarantee that every letter written to the author can be answered, but all will be forwarded. Please write to:

Robert M. Place
℅ Llewellyn Worldwide
P.O. Box 64383, Dept. 0-7387-0116-5
St. Paul, MN 55164-0383, U.S.A.
Please enclose a self-addressed stamped envelope for reply,
or $1.00 to cover costs. If outside U.S.A., enclose
international postal reply coupon.

Many of Llewellyn's authors have websites with additional information and resources. For more information, please visit our website at http://www.llewellyn.com.

ROBERT M. PLACE

A GNOSTIC BOOK OF

SAINTS

2001
Llewellyn Publications
St. Paul, Minnesota 55164-0383, U.S.A.

First Edition
First Printing, 2001

Book design and editing by Joanna Willis
Cover design by Lynne Menturweck
Illustration on page 20 based on original from *The Graphic Work of Peter Bruegel the Elder* by H. Arthur Klein, Dover Publications
Illustration on page 57 from *The Complete Woodcuts of Albrecht Dürer,* Dover Publications
Illustrations on pages 21, 36, 48, 50, 51, 53, 55, and 59 by Robert M. Place

Library of Congress Cataloging-in-Publication Data
Place, Robert Michael.
A gnostic book of saints / Robert M. Place.—1st ed.
p. cm.
ISBN 0-7387-0116-5
1. Tarot. 2. Saints—Miscellanea. I. Title.

BF1879.T2 P55 2001
133.3'2424—dc21

2001029722

Llewellyn Worldwide does not participate in, endorse, or have any authority or responsibility concerning private business transactions between our authors and the public.
All mail addressed to the author is forwarded but the publisher cannot, unless specifically instructed by the author, give out an address or phone number.
Any Internet references contained in this work are current at publication time, but the publisher cannot guarantee that a specific location will continue to be maintained. Please refer to the publisher's website for links to authors' websites and other sources.

Llewellyn Publications
A Division of Llewellyn Worldwide, Ltd.
P.O. Box 64383, Dept. 0-7387-0116-5
St. Paul, MN 55164-0383, U.S.A.
www.llewellyn.com

 Printed in the United States of America on recycled paper

I dedicate this book to my father,
Robert J. Place,
who introduced me to the saints,
and to
Archbishop Gerard Greeley,
who performed my wedding in his garage converted into
a chapel at St. Philomena's Monastery.

CONTENTS

CHAPTER 5
THE FOURFOLD WORLD
147

CHAPTER 6
THE MINOR SUITS
155

CHAPTER 7
DIVINATION
229

FOREWORD

Tarot literature can largely be divided into two classes. The first class contains academic studies of the history of Tarot. These academic studies may be meticulously accurate but offer little insight into the meaning of the symbols. The second class focuses on esoteric interpretations but seldom wastes much effort on historical accuracy. The reader is faced with a choice between meaningless fact or suggestive error.

A Gnostic Book of Saints bridges this dichotomy. Robert M. Place is a scholar who grounds his interpretations on what we actually know about Tarot history. But the focus is on the symbolic system and its meaning. The result is a readable and scholarly essay based on historical evidence rather than occult dogma.

There is little, if any, consensus on the original meaning of the Tarot symbols and considerable room for personal meditation and interpretation. In this book, Place presents the results of his own personal explorations. Some of the interpretations may strike the reader as idiosyncratic and there is no need to accept everything as gospel. But the reader will find here a deep well of insight, challenging to one's intellect and inspiring to one's intuition.

ROBERT V. O'NEILL
Author of *Tarot Symbolism*

PREFACE

My involvement with the Tarot began with a dream, and since that night, dreams, visions, and synchronicity have guided me deeper and deeper into its mysteries.

On a summer night in 1982, I had a dream in which I was walking through a room when the telephone rang. The telephone was part of the dream, but its ringing woke me into lucidity while I continued dreaming. (Buildings in dreams are often symbols of one's consciousness or ego. In this context, the telephone became a symbol of something reaching me from outside the building—from beyond my consciousness.)

With unusual clarity, I picked up the telephone. On the other end an international operator informed me that she had a person-to-person call for me from a law firm in England. I accepted the call, and then a secretary from the firm came on the line. She told me that she was sending me my ancestral inheritance. She could not tell me what it was, or who the ancestor was, only that the gift contained a power that had to be used wisely. My ancestor, it seemed, had not always done so, and to accept the gift I had to agree to accept some of his karmic debt as well. Without hesitation, I agreed. Then the secretary informed me that the gift would come from England, it was kept in a box, and that it was sometimes called "the key." She added that I would know it when I saw it.

I awoke that morning expecting to see the box at the foot of my bed. However, I had to wait several days before receiving my inheritance. That week a friend came over with his new deck of Tarot cards. As he walked through the door, my head seemed to turn involuntarily toward him, and my eyes, also acting on their own, focused on the box in his hand. I immediately recognized it. It was the deck designed in England in 1910 by Arthur Edward Waite and Pamela Colman Smith. Although I was not unfamiliar with this deck, I now saw it in a new light—I knew that this was the inheritance.

Within a few days, another friend gave me a deck called the *Tarot of Marseilles*. That was my first deck, but soon I went into Manhattan to buy the Waite-Smith cards.

Since that time, I have designed three Tarot decks of my own—this being the third—and each time the project was preceded by a dream or vision. I worked on the books for my first two decks with my friend Rosemary Ellen Guiley. In 1995, after the first two projects were in print, Rosemary suggested to me the idea of making a Tarot based on holy cards depicting saints. I was ambivalent about the idea at first, but within a few weeks I had a dream that changed my mind.

In the dream it was summer. I was walking past the ruins of an abandoned church. I was brought up Catholic, and although I have not been active with the Church for many years, I have a deep love for the beauty of Christian art and often stop to investigate churches. Therefore, it seemed natural in the dream when I decided to investigate the ruins. The door and all the windows of the church were boarded up but a basement window to the left of the stairway had some loose boards. I pulled them off and slipped in feet first. Inside there was mostly rubble from the caved-in roof, and not much was left of the side walls except for a few gaping Gothic openings where windows were once installed. I was disappointed not to find any stained glass, paintings, or statues left, but what did I expect? The church was in ruins. I sorted through the rubble, and eventually made my way to the altar—a large rectangular block of marble that was covered with dust and debris. I noticed something behind the altar and began to dig. To my amazement, I found a corpse. Not a fresh one, but the body of someone that looked like they had been dead for centuries. It was black and skeletal, dried out and easy to lift. I decided to take it home with me.

I was wondering if someone would stop me on the way, but no one seemed to mind that I was carrying a corpse. I brought it into my house and took it into the kitchen, the modern alchemical lab. At first I decided to keep it in the refrigerator, but the body caused trouble in there. It refused to stay put and contaminated other items, some of which mixed with it and caused a volatile reaction. In desperation, I decided that I should cook the body. If it did not do well with cold, maybe it needed heat. I put the body in a large pot on the stove and lit the flame. As it heated, it began to melt into black goo and ran over the top of the pot and onto the stove. This was worse than before. I tried to block it from streaming onto the floor and succeeded only in covering my hand with black goo. At this point, I wondered what this mess I was cooking tasted like. I put a sticky black finger in my mouth, and to my amazement, I tasted the most exquisite chocolate.

As I awoke, I began to realize that the corpse was the relic of a saint that had been entombed in the altar, but I was still puzzled by it turning into chocolate when I cooked it. That is, until I remembered that the Latin name for the cacao tree, the source of chocolate, is *Theobroma,* which means "the food of God."

I wish to thank my wife for her encouragement; Rosemary Ellen Guiley for first suggesting the idea; Robert O'Neill and Tom Tadford Little for their untiring investigation into the history of the Tarot; Khier for providing the quotation from St. Augustine; Barbara Wright, product development coordinator at Llewellyn, for her patience and encouragement; Joanna Willis, my editor, for her diligence and helpful suggestions; and Lynne Menturweck, the art director at Llewellyn, for her skill and consideration in handling the art.

CHAPTER 1

THE ORIGIN OF THE TAROT

A sense of fascination, mystery, awe, and at times fear surrounds the Tarot. The Tarot is a deck of cards—pictures on paper—and a modern tool for intuition. But originally, it was more often used for playing a game. The Tarot consists of seventy-eight cards divided into five suits. The four suits known as the *minor arcana* are related to common playing cards. Each suit contains ten *pip,* or number cards, and four, instead of three, royal cards. The suit symbols are the same as the ones used for playing cards in Spain and parts of Italy—staffs, swords, coins, and cups—instead of the French and English clubs, spades, diamonds, and hearts. The other twenty-two cards, known as the *major arcana,* consist of an unnumbered fool card and twenty-one *trumps*—a parade of enigmatic images, each one triumphing over its predecessor. Judging by the caliber of its participants—from the Magician to the Soul of the World—this suit seems to tell a story, an allegory of philosophical and mystical importance.

AN EIGHTEENTH-CENTURY SAVANT

Nineteenth-century occultists, such as Eliphas Levi, Paul Christian, and Papus, considered the Tarot an indispensable component of their

1

tradition, and each of them invented imaginative scenarios explaining its creation and history. However, all occult theories can be traced to the work of one man: Antoine Court de Gebelin (c.1724–1784), a Protestant pastor, Freemason, and author. Court de Gebelin was a Swiss citizen who lived in Paris and was a member of the Nef Soeurs Masonic Lodge, a famous Parisian lodge that included Voltaire and Benjamin Franklin among its members.

In 1772, Court de Gebelin sent out invitations for subscriptions to his principal work—a nine-volume encyclopedia of his observations titled *Monde Primitif* ("Primitive World"). He received over a thousand subscriptions, and worked on *Monde Primitif* until the end of his life. If he had lived longer, the work would have undoubtedly contained more volumes. The word *primitive* in the title is meant to convey the image of an initial or original world, not a savage or an uncivilized one. The work is based on his belief that before modern civilizations came into existence there was a golden age, a time when one civilization ruled the world with one language and one religion based on true wisdom. His belief can be related to the myth of the beginning time, the time when the gods walked on the earth, an archetypal golden age found in the origin myths of most cultures. Court de Gebelin tried to prove that this myth was a historic reality.

In his tomes, Court de Gebelin attempted to discover the nature of this initial world by analyzing the myths and languages of modern cultures. Although on the surface his methods seem sound, he tended to rely on intuitive guesswork more than scholarship and freely made up facts to fit his theories. As a result, most of what he wrote has been disproved, and his entire work would have been forgotten if it were not for two short essays on the Tarot that started on page 365 of volume eight. He wrote the first essay, and the second was written by a mysterious friend called the Comte de M.

Court de Gebelin said in his essay that the Tarot symbols were fragments of an ancient Egyptian book. The second writer, who is believed to be the Comte de Mellet, identified it as the *Book of Thoth*, a key link between the ancient, root culture of the Egyptians and the masters of the golden age, a book "that escaped the flames which devoured their superb libraries, and which contains their purest doctrines."[1] Thoth—portrayed as having the head either of an ibis or a baboon—was the Egyptian god of magic, writing, healing, arithmetic, astrology, and alchemy. Egyptian mythology credits him with creating the universe, ruling Egypt for 3,226 years in the mythic golden age, and then going on to rule the moon. During his reign, it is said that he invented all the arts and sciences, transmitted his wisdom to humanity, and invented writing to preserve his teachings. The Greeks equated Thoth with their god Hermes, the messenger of the gods who also was credited with the invention of writing and the transmission of wisdom. In Hellenistic Egypt, after the time of Alexander the Great when the Greek Ptolemys ruled Egypt, the two gods were amalgamated into one named Hermes Trismegistus ("Hermes the Thrice Great").

Mystic followers of Hermes Trismegistus living in Alexandria, the capital of Roman Egypt, in the first centuries of the common era believed that he was the true source of their wisdom. When they wrote, they felt that the words came from their god—we might say that they were channeling Hermes. In recognition of this fact, they signed their written works with his name. These anonymous authors' works, which were written in Greek, became keystones in the mystical teachings of the Western world.

Later in medieval and Renaissance Europe, scholars were no longer aware that these authors only credited their work to Hermes. They believed that Hermes was the name of a historic person. They believed that he was the author of the ancient works that included the oldest books on alchemy and magic and a collection of mystical philosophical texts known as the *Hermetica*. They equated Hermes with Enoch or a non-Jewish prophet, one who foresaw the teachings of Christ. They believed that the great philosophers Pythagoras, Plato, and Plotinus were transmitting a wisdom tradition founded by him, and that the *Hermetica* was as old as the Bible.

The *Hermetica* is a collection of twenty texts written from the first to the third centuries C.E.—after the time of Pythagoras, Plato, and Christ. In these texts, Hermes is presented as a man who lived long ago in the golden age when the god Ammon was pharaoh. Through mystical practices, Hermes attained gnosis and became a god. The word *gnosis* means "knowledge," but it is an experiential spiritual knowledge that differs from book learning. Gnosis is a knowledge that transforms, an enlightenment that changes one into a god. The Hermeticists were members of the polytheistic religions of Egypt and Greece. Although they believed in one supreme being that was the origin of all creation, they also believed in numerous lesser beings that they also called gods. Through the attainment of gnosis, they believed that it was possible to join the ranks of these immortals, and the *Hermetica* was a textbook that taught this procedure—a guide-book to gnosis.

In Christian terms, what the Hermeticists called gods can be equated to angels, and the heroic mystics that joined their ranks through the experience of gnosis would be called saints. Many early Christians also strove for gnosis, finding that the experience would make them one with Christ. In recognition of this fact, we call these Christian mystics *Gnostics*. The techniques used by the Hermeticists and Christian Gnostics included retreats into the wilderness to practice seclusion, meditation, and philosophical contemplation—practices that we associate with the early saints.

It was believed that the Greek *Hermetica* was derived from older texts written in hieroglyphics, the sacred writing of Egypt. This picture writing could only be deciphered by the priests of Egypt, and this fact captured the imaginations of scholars from the classical to the Renaissance worlds. They reasoned that if the *Hermetica* was a renowned source of mystical wisdom, even greater secrets were probably contained in these mysterious picture texts.

By 1614, Isaac Casauban had proven that the *Hermetica* did not predate the first century C.E. As a result, the status of this mystical text declined. However, until the Rosetta stone was discovered in 1799 and deciphered by Champollion in 1832, hieroglyphics remained a total mystery. The fact that hieroglyphics remained indecipherable allowed the myth of an ancient hieroglyphic text, the true source of Hermetic wisdom, to continue. It was this hieroglyphic book, the *Book of Thoth,* that Court de Gebelin and de Mellet believed they had found in the Tarot.

Court de Gebelin said he stumbled upon the Tarot and uncovered its Egyptian origins by accident while calling upon an unnamed countess. He visited her at her home, and found her playing a game with Tarot cards. When she laid out the World card, Court de Gebelin said, he immediately recognized it as an Egyptian allegory that had survived the ravages of time in this humble form. He then went on to explain the significance of every trump to her and her guests and declared the Tarot Egyptian. It seems that Court de Gebelin intuitively recognized that the story illustrated by the Tarot trumps was Hermetic, and because Hermetic philosophy stemmed from Egypt, he assumed that the cards did as well.[2]

While the two essays that Court de Gebelin published on the Tarot—his and de Mellet's—agree that the Tarot is of Egyptian origin, they do not concur on other details of its history. From this, we may surmise that Court de Gebelin did not think that his own theory was the final word, and to give a more complete picture of the possibilities he published his friend's alternative scenario alongside his own. For example, Court de Gebelin said that the word *Tarot* was derived from two Egyptian words: *tar,* meaning "road," and *ro,* meaning "royal." The Tarot, he said, represented the "royal road" to wisdom. De Mellet, on the other hand, said that the derivation of *Tarot* was the Egyptian *ta-rosh,* which he believed meant "the doctrine or science of Thoth."

As mentioned above, the Rosetta stone had not yet been discovered, but when it was, both assertions were proven false. The cards were named *Tarot* in French, and the English, having learned of the deck from the French, called it this also. The French name is most likely derived from the Italian *Tarocchi.* Similarly, the German name of the deck is *Tarock,* a shortened form of the Italian. Modern historians have shown that the oldest decks are Italian and that the oldest name for the deck is *Carte da Triumphi.*

According to de Gebelin, the Egyptian sages disguised their sacred book as a deck of cards and devised a card game with it to ensure that their wisdom would be preserved. This game, he said, was passed on to the Romans during the time of the empire. The game remained in Italy until the papacy was temporarily moved to Avignon in southern France in the fourteenth century. It then took root in Provence and was simultaneously picked up by the Germans. Alternatively, de Gebelin suggested that it may have been the Gypsies who introduced the Tarot to Europe. At that time, it was believed that these nomadic tribes originally came from Egypt—hence their name in English. Historians in the next century would trace the roots of the Gypsies to India instead and show that they arrived in the West too late to have introduced the cards.

Court de Gebelin also stated that each card is a hieroglyph, a sacred form of writing, and for the first time made the connection between the twenty-two cards in the fifth suit and the twenty-two letters of the Hebrew alphabet. In his essay, de Mellet also suggested that there was a connection between the Tarot and the Hebrew alphabet, but he added the Kabbalah to the mix. His main contribution is a description of how these hieroglyphs are used in divination, and a detailed exposition of the Hermetic story contained in the trumps. Reading backwards through the trumps from the World to the Fool, de Mellet shows us how the cards express the history of the world in hieroglyphs.

Because of his Hermetic background, de Mellet considered seven a sacred number. He noticed that each of the minor suits contains two times seven cards and that the twenty-one trumps can be divided into three groups of seven. He said that the first group, starting with the World card, illustrated the creation of the world and the golden age. He interpreted the Judgement card as the creation of man and woman, with the people on the card arising from the earth instead of the grave.

This was followed by cards depicting the creation of the sun (with the union of man and woman on the lower half), the moon (also showing the creation of animals), and the stars (showing the creation of sea life). The Tower depicts the fall of man, and the Devil leads us out of this golden age. The second group of seven—or the second age, the age of silver—is dominated by images of time and death. It is the stage when death and suffering are introduced, but it also contains the cardinal virtues. In the last group—the iron age—the chariot of war is followed by sexual desire (the Lovers), the temporal rulers the Emperor and Empress are surrounded by Jupiter and Juno (the Pope and Papesse), and the Magician, a deceptive trickster, leads us to the present fallen state of man represented by the Fool.[3]

De Mellet's story is well founded in Hermetic philosophy. What was left unsaid but implied in his essay is that the trumps outline the decent of humans into a state of ignorance. Therefore, when we read them in the forward direction from one to twenty-one, they describe the mystical process back to the initial state of spiritual oneness. Like the *Hermetica,* they are a textbook for experiencing gnosis.

Court de Gebelin's and de Mellet's theories had an enormous Romantic appeal and became quite popular, despite the fact that they were never substantiated. Nonetheless, fortunetellers and occultists reiterated the story of the Tarot's Egyptian origin long after the Rosetta stone was found and deciphered. Inspired by de Gebelin, the Parisian occultist Etteilla created his own Tarot designed to recapture the deck's supposed original Egyptian flavor and was to be used primarily for divination. Etteilla did much to popularize this use of the Tarot. The facts do not bear out Court de Gebelin's history, but, as we will see, they do give support to some of his and de Mellet's philosophical insights.

The Facts About Cards

Cards depend on the unique artistic material paper for their existence. Paper is light and thin, holds its shape well, and does not fray at the edges. Paper can be painted or drawn on, but it also accepts ink from printing plates. Prints are an inexpensive means of production when compared to painting and hand lettering. Before the craft of papermaking was introduced into Europe, most people could not afford pictures or books. With the production of paper came an increase in production of books and images. More and more people learned to read, knowledge was more widely disseminated, and new games and pastimes that made use of printed images developed.

The ancient Egyptians had papyrus and in the Hellenistic period they developed parchment and vellum, but none of these materials lent themselves to the creation of cards. The first people in the world to have cards were the Chinese because they were the first to have paper. The creation of paper is accredited to Ts'ai Lun, a eunuch who served the emperor Ho Ti in the beginning of the second century. Ts'ai's involvement may be a legend, but it is true that the Chinese in this period, probably using a pulp made from the bark of the mulberry tree, first manufactured paper and continued to be the sole source of it for the next five hundred years. By the eighth century, paper had spread through Asia. At the end of the eighth century paper was introduced to Egypt, but it was not manufactured there until the year 900.[4] Having created paper, the Chinese were also the first people to make paper money. Historians believe that paper money was used not only for the stakes but also as the actual cards in the first card games.

One of the oldest known Chinese decks of cards has four suits based on paper money. They were printed on heavy paper in black ink before the twelfth century. The four suits are (1) coins, which shows one or more of the familiar circular Chinese coin with a square hole in the center; (2) strings of coins, which depicts one or more cylindrical stacks of coins (the hole in the center of the coin allows a string to hold the stack together); (3) myriads of strings of coins, which has groups of stacked coins on each card; and (4) tens of myriads of strings of coins, which, surprisingly, depicts a series of illustrations from "The Story of the River Banks," a Chinese legend about the heroic exploits of the emperor's emissary on a journey to the mountain of the Taoists in the center of the world. It is a hero's journey that includes a fight with a devilish dragon before the final reward is achieved. It is easy to see in this ancient Chinese deck a relationship with the Tarot, which also has a suit of coins and a suit depicting an allegorical story.

Another early deck of cards from Korea has eight suits, each depicting arrows with different markings. What is interesting about this deck is that arrows were also used for divination, like the yarrow stalks used with the Chinese oracle, the I Ching. A strong connection exists between games of chance and divination. In his book *Games of the Gods,* Nigel Pennick makes the case that most early games evolve out of divination techniques. For example, the common checkerboard is derived from divination grids, and dice were the most common tool for both divination and gambling in the classical world.[5]

As paper spread to Egypt and the Arabic world, new games of cards came into existence. In a museum in Istanbul there are cards from Arabic decks preserved from the fifteenth century. Named after the Mamluks, an Egyptian dynasty of Islamic rulers, the decks consisted of four suits each with ten pip cards and three, all male, court cards. The suits were scimitars, polo sticks, cups, and coins. Most scholars agree that these cards stem from an older tradition, and because of their similarity to the earliest Western cards—with their suits of swords, staffs, cups, and coins—and the fact that the Arabs introduced papermaking into Europe, they are the most likely source of inspiration for Western cards.

The first evidence of card games in Christian Europe is a decree that banned a game in Bern, Switzerland, in 1367. At that time, as now, restrictions on gambling were common. Before this time, mention of cards is conspicuously absent from any lists of games or bans, but after this date, the evidence shows that cards quickly spread through Italy, France, Spain, Switzerland, Belgium, and Germany.[6]

As the game spread, card makers created new imaginative suit symbols—from acorns and bells to wild men and hounds—but eventually each country developed a standard set. The cards were called *naibbe, nahipi, nabi,* or *napis* (names that were possibly derived from Arabic), and they mostly consisted of decks of fifty-two or fifty-six cards divided into four suits—much like a modern deck of playing cards. In each suit there were ten pip cards, which simply depicted repetitions of the suit symbol corresponding to its number, and three or four court cards, which in their most complete form in some German decks pictured a jack or squire, a knight, a queen, and a king (a clear hierarchy of rank, as in feudal society: the squire is the apprentice to the knight, the knight in true chivalrous fashion is pledged to serve the queen, and she in turn to serve the king). These were clearly not Tarot decks.

The two skills that are needed for making printing plates—wood block carving and metal engraving—were practiced in western Europe during the Middle Ages. The thing that was missing for creating prints was paper. In the Middle Ages, wood block carvers used their blocks to print designs on cloth.

The wood block carvers were in either the carpenter's guild or the textile guild. The engravers, who used their skill to decorate jewelry, armor, and other metal objects, tended to be considered a higher class. They might have been in the goldsmith's guild or the silversmith's guild. Illuminators could work independently or be in the goldsmith's guild. The people who drew and engraved were in a higher class than the woodcutters.

Then in the 1300s, the Arabs supplied the missing element—paper—and the craft of making it. All the examples that we have of early hand-drawn cards and printed cards are from the 1440s on. The hand-drawn and printed cards exist side by side so we cannot say for sure which were produced first, but it is assumed that the drawn ones were first. But even the hand-drawn cards made use of production techniques such as stencils and templates that blurs the distinction between the two. The demand for paper prints brought together the skills of the illuminator with the engraver or the woodcutter.

In the 1400s, new printer's guilds began to form. In these guilds was a hierarchy, with the illustrators at the top, the cutter or engraver below them, and the workers who inked the plates on the bottom. The illuminator ran the guild and drew the designs. It is believed that he drew them directly on the plate. Then the cutter cut the plate. Many of the engraved cards and woodcuts from the 1400s tend to rival the hand-drawn cards in skill. The artists were clearly well trained and talented.

From 1450 to 1500, especially after the invention of movable type, the printing business grew by leaps and bounds. With such a demand for cards, less highly trained artists began to become involved. The cards became cheaper as they were mass-produced to supply the growing audience. Where the illuminators of the fourteenth century made books with text as well as images, many of the new printers specialized in cards.

And it was not just playing cards that the new printers made; they found a growing market for cards with pictures of saints to sell to pilgrims. For the first time, common people could not only view the great works of art in the cathedrals, but they could also afford to take an image home with them. The artists who supplied this religious market were the same artists who made decks of cards for gambling. They were experts on symbolism who had to know iconography for their saints cards, and heraldry for the work they did for royalty (some decks even used heraldic symbols for suit symbols). It is not surprising that we find religious imagery in playing cards from this time.[7]

THE BIRTH OF THE TAROT

The first Tarot deck was created in northern Italy when an unknown designer added a fifth suit containing twenty-two allegorical figures to the already existing deck of cards. The date was around 1430. The first written record of the Tarot is from 1442 from the court records in Ferrara, and the oldest existing Tarot cards are the decks that were hand-painted, with gold leaf backgrounds, for the Visconti-Sforza family, the rulers of Milan. These are dated circa 1445.

Northern Italy in the fifteenth century was a patchwork of city-states that had been part of the Holy Roman Empire since the time of

Charlemagne. But in the fifteenth century, the emperor's power out-side of Germany was declining, as was that of the pope's in the area, and the city-states, although prosperous, were fiercely independent and often at war with one another. According to historian Michael Dummett, the three cities that are most likely the birthplace of the Tarot are Milan, Ferrara, or Bologna. These cities were all centers for the manufacturing of cards, and can display the earliest documentary evidence of their existence.[8]

From the beginning, the main purpose of the deck was for playing a card game in which the cards in the fifth suit acted as trumps for taking tricks, as in its English descendant, the game of bridge. In fact, the English word *trump* is derived from the original Italian name for this suit, *trionfi*, which means "triumph." The entire deck was called *Carte da Trionfi*, meaning "a deck of cards with triumphs added."

Around 1530, *Carte da Trionfi* was changed to *Tarocchi*. The most likely reason for the change is that the game of triumphs was starting to be played with an ordinary playing-card deck in which the players would assign the status of trump to one of the four suits. Therefore, *triumphs* (*trumps*) became an ambiguous term, and a new name was needed for the five-suited deck. No one is sure what the name *Tarocchi* means, but one inspired guess is that it is derived from the name of the Taro, a river that runs through northern Italy and that was the prime source of power for early paper mills.

In the earliest decks, none of the trump cards bear numbers; the players were expected to remember the order. From lists of trumps in sermons and other literature and from the earliest numbered cards, we can determine that there were three main groups of different orders, with each of the trumps being assigned a different number in each order. At first this would seem to be disruptive to the allegory, but most of the changes are minor and have little effect on the story. For example, the four temporal rulers in the first section—the Papesse, Empress, Emperor, and Pope—may switch their order with each other but still remain together in the first section. And the last two cards, Judgement and the World, may swap places with each other. The cards that make the biggest change in location are the three virtues (Justice, Strength, and Temperance). They may be grouped together in the middle section or spread out one to each section, but again, this makes only minor changes to the allegory.

Not all of the early Tarot decks follow the standard allegory. The fifteenth-century engraved Sola Busca deck depicts various mythical and historic heroes on each of the trumps. The Florentine deck, created circa 1530, expanded the number of trumps to forty plus the Fool. This was accomplished by changing the four temporal rulers to three—the Grand Duke, the Western Emperor, and the Eastern Emperor—and then adding the other four virtues of Prudence, Faith, Hope, and Charity (there is evidence that one of the early hand-painted Milanese decks contained all seven of the virtues as well), the four elements, and the twelve signs of the zodiac. This deck came to be called the *Minchiate*. It spread through central Italy and down to Sicily but it was not produced outside of Italy until modern times.

Because it is the nature of games to demand conformity, the order of the trumps became standardized. However, because of the independence of the Italian city-states, each city-state tended to develop its own standard order. In the early fifteenth century, the Tarot spread to France and Switzerland as a result of the French invasion of Milan. Therefore, it was the Milan order that first left Italy. Marseilles, France, became a major production center of Tarot decks and introduced the Tarot to other parts of Europe. The Marseilles producers somewhat revised the Milan ordering, and this came to be considered standard to most of the world. It is the Marseilles order that is used and referred to in this book.

What makes a deck of cards a Tarot deck is the fifth suit called *trumps* or *triumphs,* which is composed of twenty-one symbolic figures organized in an ascending order. These are the cards that most people find intriguing today. To understand why the Renaissance artist would choose to add these seemingly strange figures to a deck of playing cards, we have to examine certain traditions and trends that influenced that time.

WRITING WITH SYMBOLS

The Renaissance—a name that means "rebirth"—saw the rebirth of classical wisdom and culture. The Renaissance strove to reclaim the ancients' mastery of the arts and sciences. In doing so, they reclaimed classical mysticism as well, and created a synthesis of Pagan and Christian art and philosophy.

One classical discipline that it is essential to be familiar with to understand the Tarot is the memory arts. In the classical world, the memory arts (*ars memoria*) were an essential part of the study of rhetoric; it was the discipline that helped one remember the points in a speech, or retain facts for a debate. The memory arts remained an essential part of education until the Renaissance, when the invention of the printing press made books more available to students.

Because pictures are more easily retained by the mind and incorporate many ideas simultaneously, the ancient texts recommended that the student create memory images that could be associated with each subject. It was specified that these images should be striking and dramatic. They could be unusual, vividly colored, ugly, frightening, or extremely beautiful. All students were instructed to develop memory images of their own that could be easily associated with the facts of their subject. As can be demonstrated by the modern psychological technique called *active imagination* (a Jungian therapy that employs the conscious visualization of and interaction with images from the unconscious), this imaging could easily evolve into a type of meditation that not only helped one retain information, but could heal the psyche. Over time, this art naturally became associated with magic and mysticism.

Throughout the Middle Ages, strange images called *notae* or *ars notoria* were commonly used by magicians and scholars. Notae were vivid images and were usually based on astrological symbols that the magician visualized while reciting incantations. Because images contain within them information that can be recalled and activated by visualization, medieval scholars and magicians found that power could be projected into higher realms of consciousness by manipulating these images. They felt that this power enabled them to contact presences in other planes of existence. The magicians might also have been influenced by orthodox Christian techniques of prayer and meditation that focused on icons of the saints.

In the Middle Ages and Renaissance, mystics commonly enlisted the aid of the memory arts in their quests for union with God. For example, medieval theologians Albertus Magnus (c.1193–1280) and Thomas Aquinas (1225–1274) advocated the art of memory as a "moral and religious duty."[9] In their systems, Albertus and Aquinas recommended seclusion in a dark, quiet place where one could contemplate the images of the mind undisturbed. Both authors stressed the necessity of ordering the memory images so that they followed one another in a natural progression, allowing the mystic to climb them as if they were the rungs of a ladder leading back to the Creator. The images they recommended included both the sinful and virtuous arranged in order so that the good triumphed over the bad. Images of saints were often used as virtuous symbols. Aquinas made use of images of the seven virtues, seven vices, and seven arts ordered in a way that he felt helped one ascend to God. To understand Aquinas's system it is necessary to understand the mystical concept of *emanation.*

Plato called the attainment of spiritual knowledge *anamnesis,* or "ceasing to forget," implying that this wisdom has always been with us and we need to remember it. At the core of all memory Plato placed the "Prime Mover," the first cause that started the chain of events that created the known world. Plato identified the Prime Mover with the highest spiritual ideals. He called it "the One," "the Good," and "the Beautiful," and believed that the practice of memory arts would bring one to the realization of these principles.

Philosophers in the classical world were profoundly influenced by Plato. In the first few centuries after Christ's birth, two schools of philosophy developed in which the mystical aspects of Plato's work were emphasized. These schools of philosophy are called *Neoplatonism* and *Hermeticism.* In these teachings, the One, the Prime Mover, or God is believed to create the world by transforming itself into a series of lesser gods or beings called *emanations*. It was believed that the One used these emanations like a ladder to allow the life force, or creative principle, to descend and to create the material plane, and that a mystic could make use of visualizations of these emanations to ascend the ladder back to the One.

Neoplatonic and Hermetic philosophy are at the root of most Western mystical traditions. For example, the Jewish teachings called the *Kabbalah* (which is a synthesis of this mysticism with Jewish religion) outline a version of these emanations in the Tree of Life, a meditative design that depicts ten spheres called *sephiroth*. The design is likened to a tree descending from above whose roots are in heaven. The mystic makes use of the memory arts by at first visualizing vivid images for each emanation, and then visualizing the entire structure in order to ascend back up the ladder to reunite with the creator. A similar technique was developed by the Spanish mystic Ramon Lull (1232–c.1315) who attempted to Christianize Sufi mysticism (a synthesis of Hermeticism and the Islamic religion). It is this same mystical endeavor that we find in the writings of Albertus Magus and Thomas Aquinas, and through them and other sources it was passed on to the mystics of the Renaissance.

Memory images originally were intended to be personal and kept solely in the mind. In the Renaissance, however, these vivid images were captured in enigmatic illustrations designed to aid in teaching. By 1400, when woodblock prints were being used to reproduce pictures on cards and in books, these visual aids were popular. Thus, in 1422 the climate was right for the sensation created by a book called the *Hieroglyphica,* which had just arrived in Florence. Allegedly it was a Greek translation of an Egyptian work that explained the meaning of Egyptian hieroglyphics. In actuality it only passed on a Greek misconception. Because the ancient Greeks were unable to read hieroglyphics, they assumed that hieroglyphics were not an ordinary language but rather types of allegorical pictures that incorporated many aspects of their subject into one image and invited the viewer's interpretation (or projection). In other words, the Greeks thought hiero-glyphics were types of memory images.

The *Hieroglyphica* was translated into Latin, French, German, and Italian, and became known throughout Europe. It was a major influence in developing the Renaissance trend of symbolic engrav-ings called *emblems* or *hieroglyphs,* created by prominent artists such as Dürer, Botticelli, and Bruegel and used to encapsulate various fields of knowledge. A prime example is the study of alchemy, which reached its height in the Renaissance. Alchemical texts routinely contained numerous hieroglyphs. Often the essential instructions of the work were expressed only in these enigmatic pictures. One famous example, the *Mutus Liber* (1677), is composed of pictures with no text.

The meditation upon symbols as magical paths reached its zenith in the work of Giordano Bruno (1548–1600), the ex-Dominican friar. According to Bruno, images could be charged with emotion and will. When organized to represent the divine order of the cosmos, they could enable the magus to participate in divine power itself. Cosmic consciousness, or union with God, could be obtained by holding all the images simultaneously. This was the driving passion behind the Renaissance need to acquire knowledge of all disciplines—in other words, to become a "Renaissance man."

This mystical pursuit led to a trend among Renaissance artists to create works that organized the arts, sciences, virtues, and so on into encyclopedia-like sequences that simultaneously formed emanations on a Neoplatonic ladder of ascent. The most famous examples are Dante's *Divine Comedy* (Joseph Campbell has written a comparison of the Tarot to Dante's work), and Giotto's frescos for the Arena Chapel in Padua (these have been compared to Tarot designs by his-torian Ronald Decker). One of the best examples is the so-called *Tarocchi of Mantegna,* which is not a tarocchi but a series of prints, and is not likely to have been engraved by Mantegna. It consists of fifty images that organize the conditions of man, the arts, the sci-ences, the virtues, and cosmology. It starts with the beggar and ends

with the first cause or creation. Many of the Mantegna images corre-
late with traditional Tarot symbols. There are numerous other examples of these allegorical processions: prints, poems, and a design for a
seven-tiered theater with allegorical statues. There was even an allegorical parade called the *trionfi* and the Tarot that was first named
after that parade is another example.

A PARADE OF HIEROGLYPHS

A *triumph* (or *trionfi*) is a type of parade that originated in ancient
Rome. When a conquering general returned to the city, a triumph
would be arranged down Appian Way. The parade was organized by
rank from the lowest to the highest, starting with the captives and
ending with the general himself. By the Renaissance, the triumph
had been Christianized and the characters in the parade became symbolic. It was the custom that a triumph would be performed during
Carnival, for weddings, and other special occasions. Because the triumph was a natural way to organize characters, it became a device
used by authors and artists to present a moral allegory. Petrarch's
poem *I Trionfi* is one example.

In *I Trionfi*, Petrarch presents an allegorical procession in six parts
or three pairs. The first pair is Love and Chastity, in which a proces-
sional car carrying Cupid is seen to triumph over numerous characters including earthly rulers. Cupid's car is trumped by the car of
chastity which carries Petrarch's ideal love, Laura, accompanied by
the virtues. The similarity to the Tarot's four temporal rulers, the
Lovers, the Chariot (which in the earliest hand-painted Milanese
cards depicts a beautiful woman in the chariot), and the virtues
should be obvious. In the next section of this parade, Laura, in turn,
is triumphed over by Death, the "Grim Reaper," who, like in the
Tarot, is depicted riding over, or harvesting, the bodies of common
people, kings, and popes. He in turn is trumped by Fame, which in
the Renaissance was symbolized by an angel blowing one or two
horns. This angel is substituted for the Judgement trump in the Flo-

rentine Tarot called the Minchiate. Both angels symbolize immortality and victory over death. In Petrarch's triumph, Fame is trumped by Time symbolized by a car carrying a hunched old man with wings. This figure is similar to the earliest Tarot Hermit cards on which the figure carries an hourglass instead of a lantern. The final trump is Eternity pictured by a car holding the Holy Trinity and pulled by the Four Evangelists with their four creatures: the lion, bull, eagle, and man. I make the relationship between this image and the World card clear in my discussion of that card in chapter 3.

For another example of a triumph in art let us look at Figure 1.1, a rendering of Peter Bruegel's *Triumph of Time* with the background removed so that we may focus on the parade in the foreground. The original print was completed in 1574 from Bruegel's drawing (the artist having been dead for five years) and contained a motto in Latin on the bottom that said in translation, "Time devouring all and each." The background of the actual print contains a landscape in which the left half is barren containing a city in flames and the right half is in bloom and prosperous. This theme is repeated in the foreground in the central car with its half-barren tree.

At first glance, we can discern many similarities between this allegory and the Tarot trumps. There is the triumphant chariot or car pulled by two horses with the sun and moon on their backs. On the car, we find the figure of Saturn sitting on an hourglass similar to the one the original Tarot Hermit is shown holding. Nestled in the car is the globe of the Earth, the World, surrounded by the circle of the zodiac. Poet and scholar Robert Graves, among others, traces the origin of Fortuna's wheel to this cycle of the sun's progress through the year. Graves tells us that the Latin name *Fortuna* is derived from *Vortumna*, "she who turns the year about." The Latin goddess is related to two Greek goddesses: Tiche, the original Lady Luck who indiscriminately heaps gifts or deprivations on mortals but demands generosity from those she has favored; and Nemesis, who holds a wheel and an apple bough and dispenses punishment to the unjust.[10] Both of these goddesses are related to the wheel of time and to the virtue justice. Notice

FIGURE 1.1—Bruegel's *Triumph of Time*

how, of all the signs of the zodiac in Bruegel's drawing, the scales of
Libra, symbolizing justice, are singled out for attention. Justice is one
of the four cardinal virtues. These four virtues, which were extolled by
Pythagoras, Plato, and other ancient philosophers, received the name
cardinal from St. Ambrose in the fourth century. The word *cardinal* is
derived from the Latin root *cardo,* which means "axis." The Latin term
cardinalis originally meant the four points in space—north, south, east,
and west—and the corresponding four points of the year—the solstices
and the equinoxes—that were believed to turn the wheel of the year on
its axis.

As if to echo this circle of the year, Saturn holds in his left hand a
hieroglyph, one that is mentioned in the *Hieroglyphica.* It is a serpent
biting its tail, called the *ouroboros.* The serpent, representing time,
devours its tail just as Saturn devours his child and the triumph
devours the landscape. This car represents a moralistic view of life;
triumphing over it is the next figure, the Grim Reaper. However, the
final triumph is Fame on the elephant which represents immortality
and relates to the Judgement card.

In Renaissance art, the ouroboros was a common attribute of Saturn as the god of time. It was also common in alchemical works
where it symbolized the process of the work. Figure 1.2 depicts one

FIGURE 1.2—Alchemical ouroboros

of the oldest representations of the ouroboros in an alchemical text. It is from a third-century Coptic manuscript found in Egypt. The inscription on the page with the illustration reads, "One is all, and through it is all, and by it is all." Notice how the unified circle of the serpent is divided by its shading—half in darkness and half in light. This duality is found in Bruegel's print in the dark horse of the moon and the light horse of the sun and in the half-barren and half-foliated tree. The point of the alchemical quest was to transcend this duality of time—the duality of life and death—and find immortality in the mystical realization that the one and the many are the same. Bruegel hints at this immortality with the image of Fame, but Petrarch takes us beyond Fame to a mystical vision of sacredness. Both artists have made use of the triumph for symbolic statements about the nature of life, death, and transcendence. Their triumphs are similar but not identical. The Tarot trumps are another example of this allegory with a related mystical message. The Tarot trumps are arranged in a parade with each card in order triumphing over the one before—from the Magician, a lowly trickster, to the sacred allegory of the World card.

CHAPTER 2

MYSTICS, GNOSTICS, AND SAINTS

———————

In Western history, Christianity is often portrayed as the truth triumphing over a corrupt and spiritually vacant Paganism. It is true that Christianity came to be the dominant religion in the classical world and central to Western culture for the last two thousand years, but it achieved its victory by incorporating much of the former Pagan practices, philosophies, and beliefs. It may be more accurate to visualize Christianity as a synthesis of Jewish and classical religions, a synthesis that attempted to reconcile the conflicts between these beliefs and in doing so became a new religion. At the core of any religion is the reality of the mystical experience. Classical Paganism contained mystical practices that were as spiritually vital as any, and to understand Christian mysticism we must first examine the ancient mysteries that are at its root.

MYSTICS

In Greek mythology, Orpheus was the son of Apollo and the muse Kalliope. With such divinely gifted musicians for parents, it is not surprising that he, too, was a great musician and poet. He played a seven-stringed lyre, called a *kithara*. His songs were so masterful that it was said he would charm the animals, and when he played, even the rocks and trees would begin to dance. Orpheus is credited with founding the first mystery cult based on the worship of his father, Apollo, as the principle of order, harmony, and intelligence of the universe. In Greek, all of these Apollonian qualities were expressed with one word—*logos*—and the logos was symbolized by the sun.

A mystery is a religious practice based on a secret redemptive ritual. There are different types; some involve stages of initiation, others involve a dramatic, ecstatic communion designed to sweep away individuality for the moment and allow immersion in the spirit of the deity. The Orphic ritual, however, was connected to a philosophic and artistic teaching that was designed to transform the consciousness of the participants; that is, bring them to a personal realization of their spiritual nature. This experience was called *gnosis* in Greek. As stated in the first chapter, the closest translation for *gnosis* is the word "enlightenment," a word that also equates wisdom with light and the sun. Those who were initiated into the mysteries and led to this secret wisdom were called *mystes,* and this name is the origin of the word *mystic.* The first Christians to meet in the catacombs under Rome to share their Christian mystery identified Orpheus with Christ and painted his image with his lyre to represent Christ on the walls of their sacred chambers.

In the Orphic creation myth, the beautiful god Dionysus is born of the incestuous union of Zeus and Persephone. Zeus's wife, Hera, is jealous and wishes to destroy the child. To accomplish this she has her allies, the Titans, dismember and devour him. Of course, Zeus is heartbroken and in a fit of anger he burns the Titans to ash with a volley of lightning bolts. Only Dionysus's heart remained, and from this Zeus created a new Dionysus. However, from the ash of the Titans mixed with the devoured Dionysus, the human race was born. Therefore, the human race is part divine and beautiful like Dionysus and part vicious and material like the Titans. The purpose of the Orphic mystery was to redeem the Dionystic soul and make it the dominant influence in the lives of the devotees.

Orphism is believed to be a major source of wisdom for the philosophical school founded by Pythagoras. Many of Pythagoras's followers were poets and musicians who believed that their inspiration came directly from Orpheus; hence, like the Hermeticists of later centuries, they would sign their god's name to their work. It is argued by some that the reason no writings by Pythagoras exists is that he was one who signed his work Orpheus.

The Orphics, like Pythagoras, saw a connection between music and numerical order. This type of reasoning led to sacred geometry. Pythagoras taught that numbers had qualities as well as quantity and that geometric figures were powerful magical symbols. The circle, being connected to the sky and the cosmos, was a symbol of Dionysus, the soul. The four-sided square, which relates to the four elements, four directions, and four seasons, initiated by the solstices and equinoxes, relates to the physical world. Because of this, the process that leads to the realization that the spiritual is contained in the physical is often called "the squaring of the circle" (a phrase used to describe the alchemical process as well). Because the octagon is formed by connecting the points when a circle and square overlap, it is used in art as a reference to the squaring of the circle. This symbolism is reflected in Christian art by the octagonal shape of the Fountain of Life depicted in the center of Paradise and by the octagonal shape of the garden itself. For this reason, the octagon is also often chosen for the shape of baptismal fonts and baptisteries.

In time, numerous mystery cults developed and spread throughout Greece. When Alexandra the Great unified the Middle East into one empire, he spread Greek culture and philosophy wherever he went. Even after the empire split into separate kingdoms, Greek culture and language brought unity to the area from Egypt to India. This advantage created a modern cosmopolitan atmosphere in which travel, trade, and the exchange of ideas flourished. This period, when Greek culture was dominant in this part of the world, is called the *Hellenistic period.* The largest, richest, and most powerful city in the Hellenistic world was Alexandria, Egypt, and because of their wealth and their respect for wisdom, the rulers of Alexandria created one of the world's first great public libraries. Scholars and philosophers from all of the known world traveled to the city with its famous collection of books, and in this atmosphere, a new synthesis of Greek philosophy, the mysteries, and the religious traditions of other cultures developed.

The Hermeticists that were mentioned in chapter 1 are an example of the synthesis of Greek, Egyptian, and Jewish mysticism; scholars disagree on which ingredient in this mix is dominant, which only underscores the fact that it is a synthesis. One of the most influential philosophers of this period, Plotinus (205–269 C.E.), developed his deeply mystical understanding of Plato in Alexandria. Some surmise that his teacher, Ammonius Saccas, was a Hermeticist, which would explain why we have no texts signed with his name. Plotinus's new synthesis of Plato with this magical, mystical philosophy has come to be called *Neoplatonism,* and it gave birth to a school of philosophy with numerous disciples.

Plotinus's most prominent student was Porphyry, and Porphyry, in turn, taught Iamblichus, the founder of the Syrian school in the fourth century. Iamblichus lived during the twilight of classical Paganism in the century that would see Christianity become the official religion of the Roman Empire. Yet, he tried to reform and revive Paganism and created a mystical system based on a combination of the best of Pagan philosophy. In Pagan mystical systems the creator, referred to by Plato as "the One," "the Good," and "the Beautiful," is believed to create the world by extending itself into various lower states of being. As was stated in chapter 1, these are called *emanations,* and as they extend they form a ladder of creation. In an effort to ascend back to the One, mystics would enter a meditative state and visualize themselves climbing back up the ladder of emanation.

Plotinus said that the One was beyond all duality such as masculine and feminine and dark and light, and therefore the One is also beyond our comprehension. Human comprehension only begins with the first masculine emanation called *Nous* ("mind"), the intelligence and order of the universe. This is synonymous with Plato's world of archetypes or forms, the ideas or thoughts of the universe. Plotinus went on to say that from Nous emanates *Psyche* ("soul") the life force, a living, feminine presence in the physical world that animates the creation of Nous. In Latin, Psyche is called the *Anima Mundi* ("World Soul") and she became essential to the alchemical quest.

Iamblichus believed that the Anima Mundi entered the world of matter by descending a ladder of seven planets that had been described in the philosophy of Hermes. The word *planet* is derived from the Greek word *planetai,* which means "wanderer." To the Greeks, the wanderers were the seven celestial bodies visible to the naked eye that appeared to move independently from the constellations. They included the sun, the moon, Mercury, Venus, Mars, Jupiter, and Saturn. The ancients believed that the Earth was in the center of the cosmos and that the seven planets circled the Earth. Each orbit was thought of as a crystal sphere, one nesting inside the next with the Earth in the center. Encasing the outermost crystal was the eighth sphere of the constellations and beyond that was the home of the spirit. Pythagoras created our Western musical scale with seven notes to capture the music that these spheres made as the planets circled the Earth. The same theme is reflected in the Biblical account of the seven days of creation. This Jewish tradition gave birth to the division of the month into seven-day weeks, which were adopted by the Roman Empire and received the names of the seven planetary gods.

Every living being is animated by the soul and all souls come from the one World Soul. Each part of the one Soul has to make this journey through the seven soul centers of the cosmos, the planets. Each planet clothes the Soul in qualities—later listed by Christians as the seven virtues and seven vices—as it becomes a living individual. These soul centers are echoed within our bodies as the seven centers commonly called by their Sanskrit name, *chakras.* The journey of the soul can also be conceived of as a journey through this inner space. The astrological natal chart is designed to map this process. However, as stated above, for the mystic the process must be reversed because all life yearns to reunite with what is greater than itself. Iamblichus called this desire *eros*. In a trance state, the mystic ascends this seven-runged ladder and lets go of each quality until union with the soul can be achieved. This is gnosis. To achieve this goal Iamblichus developed a complex system of study combined with mystical techniques called *synthemata*. These techniques included chanting, ritual, and visualizations related to the memory arts.

Iamblichus never achieved his hoped-for revival of Paganism. As Christianity became dominant, the old temples were closed and their rituals died out. However, in the sixth century a Syrian Christian writer known as the Pseudo Dionysus created a synthesis of Iamblichus's system with Christianity by substituting God for the One and choirs of angels for the gods of the planets. His texts, which include *The Celestial Hierarchy, The Mystical Theology, The Ecclesiastical Hierarchy,* and *Divine Names,* were translated into Latin by the Irish scholar Eriugena and became a major component in the Christian worldview.[1] Other theologians who Christianized Neoplatonism include St. Basil, St. Gregory, St. Augustine, St. Thomas Aquinas, Ramon Lull, and Marsilio Ficino who helped initiate a revival of Neoplatonism in the Renaissance.

GNOSTICS

The people of Judea thrived on the freedom offered by the Hellenistic culture. In this time in Jewish history—known as the *Diaspora*— most Jews adopted Greek culture and spoke Greek. They migrated throughout the former empire and took full advantage of commercial opportunities. A large percentage of Alexandria's population was Jewish. Many Jews also sought the experience of gnosis, which they defined as union with God. Many scholars trace the Jewish mystical tradition known as the Kabbalah to this ancient period. Jewish Gnostics developed religious communities such as the Essenes, a group that prospered in Judea in the first century C.E. The first Christians were mostly converts from Judaism and the Greek religion. At the time, Christianity was viewed as yet another Hellenistic synthesis. It is natural that many of them were also seekers of gnosis.

Gnosticism is the modern term used to describe various unrelated groups of Christian mystics who flourished from the second to the fourth centuries, including the followers of Basilides, Marcion, Valentinus, and others. The one thing that each of these groups has in common is the search for gnosis. The lack of unity among the Gnostic groups and the similarity to the Hermeticists who also searched for gnosis has caused confusion in the use of the name *Gnostic*. Modern scholars tend to reserve the term *Gnostic* for the Christians, but this is not always the case. If we think of Gnostics in the broadest sense as seekers of gnosis from the Hellenistic period then there are three main types: Pagan, Jewish, and Christian. However, it is not always clear to which group individuals should fit. For example, the famous Nag Hammadi Gnostic texts believed to be the compilation of one community and found in Egypt in 1945 contain both Christian and Hermetic texts.

All Gnostics follow the model of the Orphics in their belief that humans are both divine and material, but their philosophical interpretation of this situation falls into two groups. They are called the *optimists* and the *pessimists,* and the optimists are more often the Hermeticists and the pessimists more often the Christians. To the pessimists the physical world is a trap or a prison for the soul. They long for the time when they will be freed from the world and their soul can be reunited with God. To the optimists the world is good and animated by the soul.

Consider this quotation from Clement of Alexandria, the second-century Christian philosopher: "The ancient theologians and priests testified that the soul is united to the body as though a certain punishment, and that it is buried in this body as a sepulchre."[2] Now compare this sentiment to this quotation from Claudianus, the fourth-century Alexandrian poet believed to be Pagan: "The soul is introduced and associated with the body by number, and by a harmony simultaneously immortal and incorporeal . . . the soul cherishes its body, because without it the soul cannot feel."[3]

In these quotations, both men believe that they are accurately expressing the ideas of the Pythagorean philosopher Philolaus, but the first views the physical world and the body as something evil that the soul longs to throw off, and the second sees the world as good and the body as a vessel that is animated and made beautiful by the soul and in turn serves the soul. In the Pythagorean and Platonic writings we can actually find a combination of both of these views.

One might assume that a belief that the world is evil would be expressed in ascetic practice. It is true that the Christian Gnostics practiced ascetic self-denial such as fasting, celibacy, and seclusion. However, Hermeticists also engaged in these practices, and some Christian Gnostics are believed to have engaged in libertine sexual practices. Asceticism in itself is not a denial of the world but a technique for changing one's focus from the sensual world to the inner spiritual world. The Christian Gnostics are considered pessimistic because they reject the world as being alien to the supreme God and incompatible with the truth as darkness is to light. In their myths they credit the creation of the world to an inferior god, the *Demiurge* (which some of them equate to God in the Old Testament), and believe that Christ was sent by the true transcendent God to redeem humanity.

Gnostics, like the Neoplatonists, believed that the true God was transcendent and could only approach the world through emanations including *aeons,* the Gnostic equivalent of angels, who ruled the seven planets. The first emanation was called *Logos.* Gnostics believed that Christ was the embodiment of this universal intelligence, and was equated to Plotinus's Nous. In the beginning, Logos existed in Heaven with his female counterpart, *Sophia,* whose name means "wisdom" and who can be equated to Psyche. She is called "the sister or bride of Christ," but through an initial catastrophe of the creation of the world she became entrapped or banished in the world of matter where she suffers and awaits redemption and reunion with Logos.

She was considered the lowest of all the divine beings as she embodied lust, and yet the highest as well (even above all the aeons or angels) as she embodied divine love. Many Gnostics equated Mary Magdalen to Sophia and considered her the bride of Christ.

To orthodox Christianity, the Gnostics were heretics. The Gnostics' pessimism contradicted the fundamental goodness of God's creation, and their plethora of creative doctrines and myths was intolerable to those who sought unity and certainty in Christian beliefs. In the fourth century when Christianity became the dominant religion in the Roman Empire, Gnostic cults were forcibly extinguished. However, their influence lives on in their influence on orthodox theology. Many prominent Church thinkers in the fourth century, such as St. Augustine, were influenced by Gnostic duality, and after this time Christianity became a mix of optimistic and pessimistic views. The Gnostic religion called *Manicheism* has survived to the present in the Middle East; St. Augustine was a member of this sect before he converted.

SAINTS

During the first century of the Christian Era, Christians were honoring other Christians who had died and prayed for their intercession. However, honoring saints is not a practice created by the Church; it was part of Christianity from the very beginning—a natural practice of Christian people.

It is natural to venerate the memory of a deceased loved one. When the deceased was someone loved by the community—especially someone who had accomplished great deeds, founded a city, or won a great victory—this veneration can turn into a cult. The ancient Greeks maintained cults for the veneration of heroes; the most famous was that of Heracles, the warrior hero who embodied the virtue fortitude. Another was Orpheus, the mystical hero who embodied the virtue wisdom. It was said that a *nimbus,* a numinous cloud of light, would appear around the heads of gods when they appeared on Earth and that heroes would also display a nimbus as their divine nature became evident. These heroes were given statuses of lesser gods. Shrines were built at the heroes' tombs, they were prayed to, and they were believed to help people in times of sickness or danger. In the Jewish tradition, although they do not officially recognize saints, prophets and holy people were similarly honored with shrines. We can find similar customs in all modern religions.

The first Christian saints were the disciples of Jesus and the martyrs, people who had given up their lives for the faith during the persecution of Christianity. These people were Christian heroes who naturally inspired devotion. After Christianity came to dominate the classical world and the persecution stopped, virgins, hermits, monks, and in time, others who led exemplary Christian lives, were honored as saints. Like the ancient heroes, the list of saints includes: warriors, like St. Joan and St. Constantine; founders, like St. Benedict and St. Basel who founded monastic orders; philosophers, like St. Ambrose and St. Augustine; and mystics, like St. Francis and St. Teresa of Avila.

Eventually, the pope was asked to formally approve of each saint. In 993, the process of canonization was instituted. From that time on to the present, official saints are ones who are canonized because they have lived holy lives and now, after death, share a beatific vision (a face-to-face experience with God), the goal of all Christian mystics. Because of this relationship with God, a saint may intercede on our behalf with miraculous results.

There are three steps to sainthood: one first becomes Venerable, then Blessed, and then a Saint. *Venerable* is the title given to a deceased person recognized as being a model of heroic virtue. The next step in the canonization process is a lengthy scrutiny that will lead to beatification if the candidate is deemed worthy. After this, the holy one is referred to as *Blessed* and limited devotions are approved. If two miracles are accredited to the blessed one (though a pope may waive these requirements), then after more scrutiny he or she may move up to the category of *Saint* and receive full veneration. The saint will be assigned a feast day on the Church calendar, which is referred to as the saint's birthday but is usually the date of the saint's death—when he or she was born into spirit.

Many early saints were simply Pagan heroes or gods who became Christianized so that their cults could persist. Others were legendary characters that developed over time. Because of this, in 1968 after an investigation into the historical reality of many saints, Pope Paul VI suppressed numerous saints by taking them off the calendar and limiting or stopping their devotion. Among the suppressed were many of the most popular saints from the Middle Ages, including St. Christopher, St. Barbara, and St. Margaret.

Because the shrines to heroes were traditionally set up at the tomb of the honored one, it was deemed necessary to have some remains of the deceased saint sealed in their altar. These pieces of the corpse are called *relics,* and in the first centuries of Christianity they were probably easy to attain for the shrines of martyrs. By the sixth century, side altars were being built in churches to honor numerous saints which created a great demand for relics. Over time, the remains of saints came to be considered more valuable than gold or gems, and at times they were stolen from one church to give to another. To satisfy this demand, three classes of relics developed: the first class were actual body parts of the saint, the second were articles of clothing or objects touched by the saint, and the third class were objects that merely touched a second-class relic. Relics have always been associated with the miraculous power of the saints.

The first saint was the Greek-speaking Jew St. Stephen who was martyred by being stoned to death in 35 C.E. Today the Roman Catholic Church lists 4,500 saints.

CHAPTER 3

A MYSTICAL INTERPRETATION
OF THE TAROT

Hermetic and Neoplatonic philosophy permeated the Renaissance, and branches of learning that grew from this root—alchemy, magic, and astrology—were considered state-of-the-art. The Tarot, which was a product of the Renaissance, encapsulated these worldviews. As was stated earlier, these philosophies teach that the spirit, or the One, is beyond comprehension and can only create the world through a series of stages or emanations such as Nous and the Anima Mundi. Below this divine pair is the seven-runged ladder of the planets. Every living being animated by the soul desires to ascend this ladder back to the One, the Good, and the Beautiful, and this is the occupation of the mystic. This same soul journey is the object of the alchemical "Great Work" or "Opus," and this is the story told by the Tarot trumps.

THE TETRACTYS

Pythagoras is well-known as an ancient Greek mathematician and the first person to call himself a philosopher, which means a lover of Sophia, who is wisdom. He lived in the sixth century B.C.E., the same time that Buddha was alive in India. In many ways, his teaching paralleled that of Buddha. Pythagoras taught that life is an endless series of reincarnations until we purify ourselves and return to the One. For purification, Pythagoras recommended moral behavior based on the four cardinal virtues, a vegetarian diet and healthful lifestyle, and contemplation of numbers, the numerical abstract qualities that underlie all physical reality. To describe this latter concept he coined the word *cosmos.*

The symbol that the Pythagoreans devised to represent this numerical intelligence of the universe consisted of a triangular arrangement of ten dots (considered the perfect number) with one at the top, two on the second layer, three on the third, and four at the base (Figure 3.1). This symbol was called the *Tetractys,* and the Pythagoreans considered it sacred. If we count the space between the layers of dots as three additional immaterial layers, together with the four material layers they form the seven stages of ascent—from the fourfold base back to the One. The ancient mysteries often instituted seven levels of initiation to correspond to these seven stages, and this was repeated in the Christian mystery by the institution of the seven sacraments.

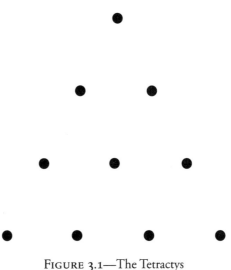

FIGURE 3.1—The Tetractys

The physical layers with the quantities of dots describe the geometric progression of the material world. The top depicts the point, a theoretical beginning with no dimension. The second layer has two points, which describe a line. Next are three points, which are necessary to form the first polygon, the triangle. The base has four points, which brings us to three-dimensional reality and allows us to form the first polyhedron, the tetrahedron (composed of four triangular sides, like a pyramid with a triangle for a base). This same progression is described in the famous alchemical quotation attributed to Maria Prophetissa: "Out of the One comes the Two, out of the Two comes Three, and from the Third come One as the Fourth."[1] If we follow this progression backward, it leads us from physical reality to its origin in the One, the Spirit.

The three immaterial layers in the Tetractys symbolized to the Pythagoreans the relationship between numbers, called *ratios*. The One contains all relationship within itself, and therefore, is beyond ratio. The first ratio is between the one and the two, written as 1:2. Between the layers in the Tetractys, we can also find the ratios 2:3 and 3:4. Pythagoras found that these ratios described the vibrations of the most important points on the musical scale: 1:2 is the whole note, 2:3 is the perfect fifth, and 3:4 is the perfect fourth. These three notes are harmonious realities that underlie all music in any culture. When we combine music and geometry we have the seven rungs of the ladder of ascent.

To fill out the scale, Pythagoras devised four other notes and created our familiar Western diatonic scale. Pythagoras believed that the seven notes of the scale captured the sound that the seven planets made as they traveled through an invisible substance called *aither* (the origin of the modern English *ether*) in their orbits. By tuning his seven-stringed lyre to this music of the spheres, he could use it to bring the corresponding soul centers in the human body into balance and health.

The four layers in the Tetractys can also be used to describe the relationships between the ratios. These are called *proportions* (proportion is one meaning of the word Logos) and they show us the evolution of consciousness back to unity. At the base we have a proportion involving four qualities, described as "A is to B as C is to D." This is written as *a:b :: c:d.* The Pythagoreans called this *discontinuous proportion.* It describes the ability to observe relationships and patterns in reality—the beginning of intelligence. Next is *continuous proportion,* involving three qualities and written as *a:b :: b:c.* This is a higher state of the perception of relationship in which the initiate begins to see the interdependence of all things. As we progress we come to a relationship of two qualities, called the *golden relationship,* in which a:b :: b:a+b. This is a relationship we can find in growth patterns in plants and animals and throughout the proportions of the human body. For example, the distance from your navel to the top of your head (a) relates to the longer distance from your feet to your navel (b) in the same proportion as the distance from your feet to your navel (b) relates to the longer distance of your overall height, from the feet to the top of the head (a+b). In the first relationship, the distance below the navel is the larger of the two. In the second this same measurement becomes the smaller of the two and relates to the larger in the same way as the smaller related to it in the first relationship. This represents the application of the dual forces of the feminine and the masculine or love and strife at work in all processes and symbolizes the mystical state approaching unity. In the final state of Oneness, all relationship is dissolved in unity.

The Neoplatonic philosopher Porphyry said in his *The Life of Pythagoras,* "Things that had a beginning, middle and end they denoted by the number Three, saying that everything that has a middle is triform, which was applied to every perfect thing. They said that if anything was perfect it would make use of this principle, and be adorned according to it; and as they had no other name for it, they invented the form triad, and whenever they tried to bring us to the knowledge of what was perfect they led us to that by the form of the triad."[2] Earlier, the philosopher Aristotle wrote, "For as the Pythagoreans say, the All and all things are defined by threes; for end and middle and beginning constitute the number of All, and also the number of the Triad."[3]

THREE STAGES

We see these same three stages in all myth, visions, and systems that describe the process back to the One. Pythagoras illustrated these stages in a story found in Iamblichus's *The Life of Pythagoras* that describes three different types of men who come to a fair. The first comes to sell his wares and sees the fair as an opportunity for profit. He is dominated by the concerns of the first three soul centers, from the sacrum to the navel. The virtue that he is developing is temperance. The second man is heroic; he comes to compete in the games and win glory. This man is dominated by the soul center of the heart, and is developing the virtue strength or courage (the word *courage* is derived from the Latin root *cor* meaning "heart"). The third man comes to the fair to observe and contemplate; he is the one Pythagoras describes as a philosopher. His concerns are of the higher three soul centers from the throat to the crown, and his virtue is prudence. This man is on the golden path, and his path leads to the union with the One.[4]

This same pattern can be seen in the theme underlying Plato's masterpiece, *The Republic*. While describing the perfect society, Plato also describes the stages necessary for the development of the philosopher king, the ruler of his utopia. To become a citizen of Plato's republic, one must develop the virtue temperance, a balance of desires achieved through the study of music. These people become the workers that form most of the population. From this pool, certain people will be able to develop the virtue strength through the study of gymnastics and rise to the level of warrior protectors. From this elite group, some will develop the virtue of prudence or wisdom through the study of math. These men and women will become the philosophers and leaders. From this group, one, who is equated to gold, will achieve union with the will of heaven and become the philosopher king or queen, the embodiment of the virtue justice.

Again, this pattern can be seen in the story of Christ as expressed in the mysteries of the rosary. The five *Joyful Mysteries* relate to the first stage, the development of peace and prosperity in the physical world. These mysteries are concerned with divine being embodied in the child who is Jesus. The second group of five is called the *Sorrowful Mysteries*. They relate to Christ's heroic sacrifice that led to the crucifixion and are concerned with the self-sacrifice and fortitude of the sacred warrior. The last five are the *Glorious Mysteries,* which describe Christ's resurrection and ascension, the assumption of the Blessed Virgin, and the attainment of wisdom and gnosis.

The influential, twelfth-century, visionary monk Joachim de Fiore saw this pattern as describing the evolution of all humanity. In his grand vision, he related all of human history with the three aspects of the Holy Trinity. In the first age, the *Age of the Father,* the physical world was created, the law was given, and the Old Testament was written. In the *Age of the Son,* Christ was born and made his heroic sacrifice to save the world; the New Testament was written and the Church began. In the coming *Age of the Holy Spirit,* the Church will be dissolved. It will be the golden age that Christ promised when love will rule and individuals will communicate directly with God.[5]

The Trumps

The threefold pattern described above is archetypal. It can be found in all cultures. The Jungian scholar Joseph Campbell called it "the hero's journey." In the Tarot, it is found in the trump cards.

In the game of Tarot, the Fool is not a trump proper, he is a wild card of no value that can fit in anywhere in the sequence. He can be thought of as taking the Fool's journey, the hero's quest. There are twenty-one numbered trumps that can be neatly divided into three groups of the mystical number seven (Joachim also divided each of his three ages into seven stages). These can be thought of as three acts.

On the first numbered trump in the Marseilles deck we find dice on the table of the *Bateleur.* This is true of most early printed decks from Italy or France. Dice were an ancient tool for divination as well as gambling, and this use of combinations of numbers can be related to Pythagorean mysticism. There are twenty-one possible combinations of the throws of two dice, and this number represents all the possible divinatory solutions that two dice can give. In the Renaissance, these twenty-one possibilities were represented in a book on divination titled the *Trionpho della Fortuna* as twenty-one allegorical figures related to the twenty-one trumps of the Tarot. Dice are designed so that the numbers on alternate sides of the die always add up to the mystical seven.[6] The Bateleur initiates the sequence of trumps; his two dice are outlining the series like a table of contents. The trumps can be thought of as a three-act play, each composed of seven cards.

The first act, which depicts couples triumphed by love, is the *Joyful;* the second act, dominated by images of time, mortality, and suffering, is the *Sorrowful;* and the third act, with its celestial ascent to the soul of the World, is the *Glorious.* These three acts represent the mystical ascent of the spirit immersed in the physical world, the world of the four elements, four directions, and four seasons represented by the four suits in the Tarot.

The same three-to-four relationship that we find in the Tetractys can be seen in each of the seven trump cards in each act. In the first act, there are four ruling figures that are paired into two couples. These figures relate to the fourfold physical world with four directions, four seasons, and four elements. The theory of the four elements can be traced to the Pythagorean philosopher Empedocles (490–430 B.C.E.). Although he was a natural philosopher, something like a physicist, he was also a mystic, and he presented his theory with this fragment from a poem: "Here first the four roots of all things: Dazzling Zeus, life-bearing Hera/Aidoneus, and Nestis who moistens the springs of mortals with her tears."[7]

In these lines, the four elements are presented as two divine couples who rule over the physical world and the afterlife. Zeus, the god of heaven, represents the air; Hera, his wife and the life-bearing mother, is earth; Aidoneus, another name for Hades, is the god of the underworld where there is fire in the earth; and Nestis is a Sicilian name for Hades' wife, Persephone, who represents water with her tears.[8] Notice how the Tarot also has two couples representing the fourfold world: the Emperor and Empress are like Zeus and Hera as the rulers of the physical world, and the Pope and Papesse are like Hades and Persephone as the rulers of the world of the soul.

Around the four are three other cards that depict the action of the first act. The Bateleur introduces the play and begins the action. The Lovers card in the oldest decks simply shows a marriage or a betrothal and clearly indicates the triumph of love over the fourfold world. After all, isn't that why they are in couples? In the Tarot of Marseilles, this card depicts a man choosing between a life of study and one of sensuality, symbolized in some of the decks as a woman with a laurel wreath and a woman with a wreath of flowers. This is the decision that every true philosopher has to face. This image can be traced to the Pythagorean allegory that describes the Greek letter upsilon (which looks like a Y) as representing two paths, one easy but leading to ruin and one difficult but leading to mastery. The final card, the Chariot, shows that our hero has resolved to take the journey to the next level, the path that takes the sorrows of the world head-on. Even in the earlier decks that depict a beautiful woman in the chariot, she represents virtue and the strength to go beyond the confines of Cupid.

The second act contains three cards that represent the human mortal condition, the suffering to which all life leads. They are the Hermit, the Hanged Man, and Death, and they symbolize old age, suffering, and death—the same three sights that Buddha had to confront to find his motivation for his mystical quest. Interspersed with this group are four cards representing the four cardinal virtues that were extolled by the classical writers. Three of the four are clearly labeled as Justice, Strength, and Temperance. Occultists in the eighteenth and nineteenth centuries, knowing that there should be four, have tried to turn the Hanged Man into Prudence, but this is a mistake. The only card left in this section to play the role of Prudence is the Wheel of Fortune, and when we understand the allegory we will see that this card is a fitting symbol for the highest virtue.

As stated in the first chapter, the virtues were first called "cardinal" by St. Ambrose, the fourth-century bishop of Milan and one of the four "Doctors of the Church." This was part of his effort to Christianize Greek philosophy. The word *cardinal* is derived from the Latin root *cardo* which refers to the axis of a wheel. *Cardinal* means "that which turns the wheel." Originally, this referred to the four directions and the four constellations of the seasonal changes, which turned the wheel of time and space. St. Ambrose used it to indicate that the virtues were more powerful than time and space.[9] This insight is Wisdom or Prudence and it is exactly what is illustrated on the Tarot of Marseilles's Wheel. Here we see the wheel of fate or time with three foolish creatures traveling around it. They represent the three follies that cause the three aspects of suffering that are placed in this second act. Notice that in the Tarot of Marseilles the cardinal virtues are in the opposite order from the way they were presented by Pythagoras and Plato. The virtues are moving against time and suffering. The symbol of the wheel is possibly derived from a Pythagorean image of the wheel of reincarnation. On the Tibetan Buddhist image of the wheel of rebirth, we can also find in its center three creatures symbolizing the folly that ties us to the material world. In this light, the virtues are leading us to the end of mortality—the immortality of mystical union.

The last act starts with two cards that can be described as bad and ends with two that can be described as good; they complement each other. In the middle are the three celestial figures the Star, the Moon, and the Sun. We start the act with the Devil in charge. The Tower breaks this power—what was crowned is toppled. Judgement allows the physical to ascend to the spiritual, and the final card, the World Soul, shows the attainment of the Good. The transition is accomplished by ascending through the seven planets depicted on the Star card as seven stars that lead to the eighth sphere represented by a large star in the center. This configuration is introduced with a nude representing truth and beauty. The Moon and Sun, although part of this group, are highlighted on separate cards because they also represent the feminine and masculine forces that form the golden relationship. Like all true philosophical quests, the cards have delivered us to the mother of our soul, the Anima Mundi, who is depicted in the center of the World card.

THE WORLD

If we are to view the Tarot trumps as a journey back to the soul, we would expect to see an image of the World Soul on the last trump, numbered twenty-one. And that is exactly what the last trump, particularly in the Tarot of Marseilles, illustrates.

When we study the religions of the world, we find common patterns of behavior and belief that the psychologist Carl Jung labeled *archetypal.* The most basic and consistent of all these archetypes is the idea of the sacredness of the center—the mythical center of the world. This is the point that orients our entire world, it is the place of origin, and the sacred place where Heaven, Earth, and the lower regions connect in myths. It may be called the "Axis Mundi," the "Navel of the World," or the "Tree of Life," but we find it in every mythology, religion, and mystical philosophy.

This place may be marked by a stone, a pole, a tree, a mountain, a city, a temple or church, or an altar with a fire reaching to Heaven. For every culture, it is different; yet, it always marks the same spot—the center of our being, what Jung calls the *Self*—it is the place of spirit.

We find it in the practices of most basic tribal people such as the nomadic Achilpa of Australia who carry a sacred pole with them during their wanderings. This pole connects them with their ancestors in the sky, and the direction in which the pole bends determines the direction the tribe will take (an early form of divination). Having the pole with them assures them that no matter where they wander they are always in the center, for they bring the center with them wherever they go.[10] Thus, they are always in contact with their ancestors. Their ideas may seem primitive to us, but the flagpole continues to serve a similar function in modern culture.

In Europe we can find references to sacred pillars among the Celts, Romans, Greeks, and Germans. In mythology, this can take on grand proportions such as Yggdrasil, the Norse world tree that connects Asgard with Middle Earth. In other major world religions it can take the form of a mountain that is the center of the world and the reflection of the heavens; this is the function of the Great Pyramid of Egypt or Mount Meru in the mythology of India. It can also be the abode of the divine, such as Mount Olympus in Greece or Mount Sinai where Moses received the Ten Commandments. To Islam it is the Kabah in Mecca, which is said to be right below the throne of Allah. To the Jews, it is Jerusalem; to the Catholics, Rome; and it is the church in the center of every small town with its steeple reaching toward Heaven.

From this central point, the world is always oriented to the four cardinal directions: north, south, east, and west. These directions define the center and help us find our way in the world. We find this orientation in all symbols of the center. In the Bible, we find this structure in Eden, from which the four rivers of the world emerge from the fountain of life in the center. The rivers are said to be the Tigris, the Euphrates, the Geon (Ganges), and the Pison (Nile). Next to the fountain in the center we find the Tree of Knowledge and the Tree of Life. According to legend, the cross of Jesus was later erected on the spot where the Tree of Knowledge once grew. This pattern is the archetypal blueprint for all temples, churches, classical gardens, and cities.

The same pattern can be found in all aspects of the physical world, such as the division of the year into four seasons, or the alchemical division of matter into four elements. Alchemists said that the four elements were unified by an unseen fifth element called the *quinta essentia,* or the "essential fifth." This is where the word *quintessence* comes from. The quinta essentia is the Anima Mundi, the feminine soul of the world. Discovering and unleashing the Anima Mundi was the sole purpose of the alchemical quest. The Anima Mundi is the divine love that permeates the world, heals it, and holds it together. She exists in the center. There is an archetypal pattern for illustrating this relationship called a *quincunx*. A quincunx is an arrangement of five elements with one at each corner and the fifth in the center. It appears in the art of all cultures, and whatever is in the center is what that culture finds sacred.

The Anima Mundi is the magic elixir for which, as Joseph Campbell points out in *The Hero with a Thousand Faces,* every hero searches. The hero's journey takes him or her through a death of the ego and a transformation that leads to the center of the world. There he or she makes the ascent to the realm of the gods and captures the healing elixir. This is why the knights of the Round Table searched for the Grail Castle, why Odin hung himself from Yggdrasil, why Buddha sat under the bo tree, and why the emperor's emissary on one of the oldest Chinese decks of cards journeys to the mountain of the Taoists in the center of the world. The quincunx acts as a map of the world and shows us where to find the center.

This same pattern is the structure of the Tarot. The four minor suits are a division of the physical world into four classes, four elements, and four directions. But their existence defines the center, the fifth suit which is the trumps where the hero's journey of death and rebirth is pictured. The final and culminating card in the traditional Tarot is the World card. This card is like a magical diagram of the entire deck. In the center of the World card is a symbolic picture of the Anima Mundi, a beautiful woman that represents the love that unites the world. Alchemists equated her to the fifth element that united the other four. Her central position is defined by the symbols assigned to each corner. Here we find the Christian symbols of the Four Evangelists: the lion, bull, eagle, and man. These symbols are commonly associated with the four directions and the four elements through their connection with the four fixed signs of the zodiac: Leo, Taurus, Scorpio, and Aquarius. When we use the Tarot to quest into our unconscious, this is what we are searching for—the love that we can find within the center of all creation and therefore in the center of our self.

The simplest way of depicting the sacred center in art is to draw or sculpt two animals coming together face-to-face. The animals may be lions, deer, birds, and so on. Between them is the symbol of sacredness: a tree, a column, or maybe a fountain. In Greek mythology, this is reflected in the myth of the founding of Delphi. It was said that Zeus let two birds fly in different directions. The two flew over the length of the Earth until they met face-to-face in the center. At this point, which was Delphi, a stone was erected and called the "Navel of the Earth." Delphi was considered the most sacred spot in Greece and became famous for its oracle. (Notice how the sacred center and divination are once again connected.)

In the oldest designs of this type we find a human figure in the center, sometimes a man but most often a woman. Archeologists call this figure the "Mistress of the Animals." She is believed to be a mother goddess. One of the most common names for the goddess was *Anna*, which is reflected in the name of the Latin goddess of the hunt, Diana. It is also the root of the Latin word for "soul"—*anima*—which is retained in the English name for her creatures—*animals*.

Figure 3.2 is a drawing of the Mistress of the Animals found on a seventh-century B.C.E. amphora from the area in central Greece called Boeotia. Although this image fits the basic pattern of sacredness by depicting animals facing the goddess in the center, it expands on the number of animals. With four prominent animals at the four corners of the design and with the large figure of the goddess in the center, it is one of the oldest examples of the quincunx. In case we did not understand the significance of this pattern, the artist has included cross forms in the background.

This goddess also displays one of the oldest uses of the symbolic shape known today as the heart. This heart shape would not be associated with the organ of the chest for another fifteen hundred years when an artist of the late Middle Ages crafted it as a symbol of love. Here it expresses in the simplest form a beautiful and loving feminine face. The goddess is beautifully dressed and has large arms held in a gesture of openness, acceptance, and support. Attracted to her are animals from

FIGURE 3.2—Mistress of the Animals

the three divisions of the world: land, air, and sea. Notice that the land animals are large carnivores, possibly lions. She offers them the meat of a slaughtered bull. On her arms are two large birds, possibly eagles, also attracted by the meat. This bears comparison to the Marseilles's World card which is also a quincunx with a beautiful woman in the center surrounded by a lion, an eagle, and a bull.

Also, notice that the slaughtered bull is represented by its head and its rear leg—its beginning and end. In Egyptian hieroglyphics we find that the concepts of above and below are expressed by the images of the head and the rear of a lion. This is likely how Hermes' famous phrase "As above so below" was originally written. In Christian art, the joining of opposites is symbolized by the Greek letters alpha and omega, the first and last letters of the alphabet. Alpha and omega symbolize Christ's victory over death. Perhaps this Greek vase contains a similar message. After all, isn't the end of the bull used to nurture the life of the carnivores, an example of death leading to life?

Figure 3.3 is a drawing of a classical relief sculpture depicting another example of a quincunx from the Orphic mysteries. In the Orphic creation myth the first being was the goddess Night. She danced and created the winds. By mating with the north wind, she fertilized a silver egg in her "womb of darkness." The north wind spiraled like a great serpent around the egg to help it hatch, and from the egg a beautiful creature of light, called Phanes or Eros, emerged. Phanes was double-sexed, golden-winged, and had four heads: that of a bull, a lion, a ram, and a serpent. Phanes created the earth, sky, sun, moon, and stars.

In the drawing we can see the radiant Phanes emerging from the egg with his serpent father still spiraled around him. Against his wings is the crescent of the moon and in his hand is the torch of the sun. In his left hand, he holds the axis mundi and the oval surrounding him contains the zodiac. The heads of the four winds in the four corners and Phanes in the center form a quincunx. However, this fourfold pattern is repeated in the four animal heads that surround his human head. The winds orient Phanes in space but the animal

FIGURE 3.3—The Orphic Phanes

heads orient him in time; they represent the four seasons. The ram was associated with Zeus and the spring, the lion with Helios and summer, the snake with Hades and winter, and the bull with Dionysus and autumn.

Figure 3.4 is a drawing of a thirteenth-century French champlevé enamle on gilded copper. It was created to be nailed to the cover of a Bible, and depicts a common Christian icon called "Christ in Majesty."

FIGURE 3.4—Christ in Majesty

From the Middle Ages on, this image appears painted in manuscripts or on church walls and ceilings, or carved on the covers of Bibles or in the tympanums over church doors. In the Christ in Majesty icon, the central figure, encased in an almond-shaped or circular aura (called a *mandorla*), is Christ dressed in white and enthroned, or he may be symbolized as a lamb. Surrounding him, one to each corner, are the four living creatures that represent the Four Evangelists of the Gospels: St. Mark, St. Luke, St. John, and St. Matthew. These images stem from Ezekiel 10:1–22 in which the Old Testament prophet describes the four "living creatures" surrounding the throne of God as each having four faces, one of each of these creatures. Reference to these four is made again in Revelation 4:6–10, where St. John sees them in a mystical vision surrounding the throne of Christ (which he also says is preceded by seven lights). Inspired by these texts, medieval artists created this icon. In doing so, they were making use of the archetypal map of the sacred. Because of their association with the four fixed signs of the zodiac, these symbols came to represent the four directions, the four elements, and the limits of the physical world animated by the presence of Christ.

Notice that to either side of Christ's head are the alpha and the omega symbols—another detail derived from Revelation. In this icon, the position of the omega suggests that the end comes before the beginning, just as Christ's death came before his resurrection and everlasting life.

Because the Christ in Majesty image is described in Revelation (a description of the Second Coming when the dead will rise and Christ will sit in judgment), this icon often appears as the central image in illustrations of the Last Judgment. However, the Christ in Majesty icon in itself is an image of the throne of Christ. It depicts him as the animating spirit that permeates the world, a world in which his evangelists spread his message to the four corners. One of the primary uses of the icon was to decorate the cover of the Bible, thereby declaring the book as the living presence of Christ in the world.

Figure 3.5 depicts an icon of the Madonna painted in Italy circa 1260 by Margarito D'Arezzo. In this image, Mary sits in the center of

FIGURE 3.5—Madonna Enthroned

the mandorla like a sacred mountain—the axis mundi herself—with the infant Christ on her lap and the symbols of the Four Evangelists in the four corners, spreading the Word to the four directions. This icon is a variation of Christ in Majesty, but here Christ is clearly being depicted as the spirit of God incarnate, as the First Coming. In this icon, Christ shares his central position with his mother. She is also the soul of the world, the animating force that has given birth to God.

When Margarito painted this panel, the cult of Mary, which had been growing in the West since the twelfth century, was at its height, and Christian mystics who embarked on an inner ascent to the Seventh Heaven were rewarded with similar visions of Mary as the Throne of God. Like an ancient mother goddess, Mary is crowned and sits on a throne carved in the image of two lions. These ancient goddess thrones were themselves derived from images of the Mistress of the Animals with her carnivorous beasts at her side. At the height of her cult, Mary has become the Anima Mundi.

Figure 3.6 depicts a mandala-like symbol representing the Philosopher's Stone from a seventeenth-century French alchemical manuscript titled *Harmonie Mystique*. This "Stone" was the most important thing in the world to an alchemist. To create it was the goal of alchemical work, a process in which the substance of the work was believed to be killed and resurrected. The final result was to be a substance of pure spirit in which the gross physical elements of the matter have been purified, leaving only the Anima Mundi. The Stone was believed to act as a catalyst, transforming whatever it contacted into its highest form. It could transform base metal into gold, cure any illness, and bring the alchemist to a higher spiritual consciousness.

To symbolize the Stone, alchemists would design a quincunx with the details determined by their own mystical vision. In the four corners they would place symbols of the four elements, and in the center, the place of the fifth element (the quinta essentia), they would devise a symbol for the Anima Mundi. The Anima Mundi might be depicted as a sacred mountain surmounted by Hermes or a fountain holding Christ, but most often it was depicted as a nude goddess.

FIGURE 3.6—The Philosopher's Stone

Alchemy was introduced to western Europe in the twelfth century and these images are prevalent in the alchemical texts of that time.

In the unique oval design of Figure 3.6 the Anima Mundi is depicted as a heart in the center of a cross with images of the four elements assigned to each quarter. A twisted thorn-covered vine closely encircles the heart. From its top, a rose bud sprouts and five drops of blood are on its front.

The heart, of course, is a reference to the sacred heart of Christ. The five drops of blood are a reference to his five wounds, which were in themselves used in a quincunx in Christian art, and the circle of thorns was his crown during his crucifixion. In Christian art the sacred heart can also be a symbol of Mary's divine love, but to distinguish hers from that of her son a rose is added. Here, like in Margarito's icon, we see both symbols combined into one. However, in this alchemical icon the rose is only a bud. In Margarito's icon, Christ is depicted as a child in his mother's lap. Here the roles are reversed: a newborn rose emerges from the symbol of Christ. The feminine is depicted as the inner soul emerging from the masculine.

Figure 3.7 is a print Albrecht Dürer created in 1502 for a humanist text on philosophy. The figure in the center of the quincunx is the goddess Sophia with her name expanded to *Philosophia*, "the love of wisdom." To make it clear that the wreath surrounding her represents the wheel of the year, its foliage illustrates seasonal changes. In the four corners we find the heads of the four winds clearly labeled with their names in the margins, their respective element, and the human temperament associated in the Renaissance with the four bodily humors. She is clearly situated in the center of time and space. At the cross-quarters of the wreath are images of four prominent philosophers: Ptolomy the Egyptian, Plato the Greek, Cicero the Latin, and Algertus the German. In the Renaissance, alchemists and other humanists reclaimed the sacred feminine principle and such humanist icons were instrumental in this process. Notice the similarity between this image and Marseilles's World card. Also, on top of the stack of books held by Sophia is a Bible, recognizable by the simplified quincunx on its cover.

It was thought that the quincunx design on Marseilles's World card with the female figure in the center developed in France in the seventeenth century, but some Tarot cards found in the walls of Sforza castle suggest that it may have an earlier history in Milan. The nude on the World card is dancing in the center of four creatures: the lion, the bull, the eagle, and man. These symbols are interchangeable with the four elements on the alchemical mandala and the four directions on Dürer's Sophia. Because it uses the creatures of the Evangelists, the

FIGURE 3.7—Dürer's Sophia

Tarot World is related to the Christ in Majesty icon. Although, with one exception, in all the decks the central figure is not Christ; it is a nude female figure. The one exception is the seventeenth-century Jacques Vievil deck. The World card from this deck is depicted on the left in Figure 3.8. In this instance, we find a male figure in the center, and because he has a halo, scepter, and cape, we may identify him as Christ in Majesty. However, other than his cape he is nude, and therefore he is still not an orthodox representation. It is as if the creators of the Tarot are telling us that what the orthodox artists have depicted is not sacred enough. The creators of the Tarot wanted to depict the real naked truth that Christ represents. In the majority of the decks, this truth takes the form of the female. Sometimes, as in the central card in Figure 3.8 from the seventeenth-century Jean Noblet deck, she can be seen wearing the cape and holding the scepter like Christ, but she represents something more—she is Christ's feminine soul. In the third card in Figure 3.8 from Heri's 1718 deck we see the most prevalent French design. The artist has designed every part of this figure to communicate beauty and femininity. Putting this beautiful nude in the center—the place of sacredness—symbolically states that she is the soul. Putting the label "World" on the bottom of the card, combined with the symbolism of the quincunx, clearly states that she is the World Soul, the goal of the mystical quest, and demonstrates that the Tarot is mystical.

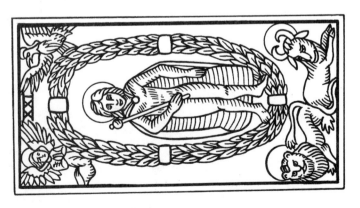

FIGURE 3.8—Seventeenth- and eighteenth-century French World cards

CHAPTER 4

A PARADE OF SAINTS

---

*T*arot of the Saints demonstrates that there is a saint to match each of the archetypal figures in the Tarot trumps. In fact, on several occasions the story of a saint seems so similar to the image on one of the trumps that it may have been the original inspiration for the card (e.g., St. Barbara and the tower). Saints and their legends were certainly familiar to the Renaissance card makers because they were also the producers of the first holy cards that pictured saints and were popular mementos for pilgrims and participants in religious events. Like the Tarot, the production of holy cards continues to thrive, and these cards were what inspired the creation of the *Tarot of the Saints*.

Although the trumps are meant to form a progression with each one triumphing over its predecessor, we find in the *Tarot of the Saints* that each saint represents a triumph in him- or herself. Each is an example of a saint's heroic victory; sometimes this struggle was with evil, but the best is when the struggle was with the saint's own inner nature and the victory was the spiritual transformation of the self.

Sometimes the stories of saints seem naive or even perverse to our modern sensibility. Almost all of the early female saints seem to prefer torture or death to the joys of sexual relations, and some saints seem to go overboard in their asceticism. Some of the early theologians and philosophers of the Church were unduly suspect of sensual pleasure and imbalanced toward a pessimistic view of the world. Many of the earliest saints are not historically real people and their stories seem to have been crafted by these Church fathers to express their moralistic messages. However, these figures are often borrowed from pre-Christian myths (even Buddha was transformed into a Christian saint), and if we read between the lines, we can find true mystical insights that explain why these legends were valued by common people for centuries.

Many saints are also powerful role models; real heroes who demonstrate love, generosity, and mystical insight. These are the saints who speak to us the strongest, who challenge us to live up to their standards, to be more loving, more giving, and more selfless.

For each card in this section there is a discussion of the life and legend of the individual saint depicted, a discussion of the history and symbolism of each trump, and a section on the divinatory meaning of the card. The information on the lives of the saints can be read in itself as a "book of saints" and will add richness to reading with the deck. The information on the trumps is provided to give insight into the origin of the Tarot's symbolism, and the divinatory meaning is provided as an aid to interpreting the card, but it is not intended to exclude individual associations. There are no reverse meanings provided. To understand the reasons for this, please refer to the beginning of chapter 7.

St. Francis ■ The Fool

If I were to see the Emperor, I would beg him to command that grain be scattered on the roads at Christmas to regale the birds, especially our sisters the larks.

St. Francis of Assisi

St. Francis of Assisi is one of the most loved of all the saints. His example of selfless devotion to others has been an inspiration to every generation. He and St. Thomas are recognized in the Hindu pantheon as healers and as enlightened masters, and he is celebrated in modern culture for his respect for animals and all of nature.

The Fool card can be viewed as the lowest of all the cards of the fifth suit. Yet in some ways, it is the most valuable. In the game of Tarot, the Fool was called the *excuse*. It could be played instead of a trump to keep the player in the game, but unlike one of the trumps, it could not win a trick. However, because of its high point value at the end of the game, it was one of the most valuable cards to hold. This humble position outside of the trumps and the competition of the game would be one that St. Francis would have chosen for himself, and in that choice he would be demonstrating his great worth. Still, it might not seem appropriate to call him a fool if it were not for the fact that he often referred to himself as an *"idiota."*

A Fool for Christ

Named Giovanni at his birth in 1181, St. Francis's name was changed to Francesco ("Frenchman") because of his mother's French heritage and his father's love of France. Francis's father was a rich merchant living in Assisi, and Francis grew to be a spoiled young man who loved drinking and listening to the songs of the troubadours. Like the legendary heroes in the songs, he dreamed of becoming a knight himself, and with his father's encouragement he tried several times to distinguish himself in battle. However, his attempts continually met with frustration. He participated in the war between Assisi and Perugia, but for him it ended with a perilous bout of illness and imprisonment. Upon his release, he attempted to participate in the war with Apulia, but illness forced him home again. Once home, he was shocked by the sight of an important general who had been reduced to begging in the streets. Francis was already tormented by his own failures and the ridicule that he suffered, but this twist of fate was more than he could bear. He entered a deep depression and wandered the countryside looking for solace.

In his youth, Francis had been terrified by the sight of leprosy. One day while wandering he came across a leper coming from the opposite direction. The voice of God told him to kiss the leper. Although he was terrified, he heeded the command and kissed the leper. When he did, his depression lifted and he began to see that the cure for his suffering was in the service of others.

On another occasion, Francis came across the ruins of a church in San Damian and fell to his knees in prayer at the foot of its abandoned cross. As he did, Christ spoke to him, saying, "Francis, repair my house." Later in life he would come to realize that Christ was asking him to repair Christianity itself. By pledging himself to poverty and service, he would be repairing the institution of the Church which, at that time, was coming under criticism for its greed and opulence. But when he first heard Christ's words he naively believed that he was only being asked to restore the ruined church at San Damian. To accomplish this, he sold some of his father's rich fabrics. This act outraged his father and caused him to disown his son. Undaunted, Francis continued to raise money for supplies by begging and began doing the construction work himself.

Francis had a gift for speaking and his sincerity, commitment, and joyous nature soon won him followers who helped in his efforts. San Damian was successfully restored, as were several other churches, and Francis and his followers wandered through the countryside begging, preaching, and administering to the sick and the poor.

When Francis had gathered a large enough following, he decided it was time to ask for papal approval for his brotherhood. He walked to Rome and presented himself to Pope Innocent III. The pope was besieged daily with such requests and had no patience for yet another reformer. Therefore, in a belligerent voice the pope commanded Francis go and preach to the pigs. Once again, Francis's foolish wisdom paid off. He took the pope's command literally and went out to find some pigs and preach to them. Pope Innocent was impressed by this act of humility and gave his approval to the new order.

Preaching to the pigs would not have sounded as absurd to Francis as the pope may have thought. He had a deep love of nature and is said to have preached to animals on numerous occasions. On one occasion, the town of Gubbio was troubled by a wolf attacking its sheep. Francis had a talk with the wolf. Afterward, the wolf changed his ways and no longer ate sheep. (A similar story was told in ancient times about Pythagoras and a bear.)

In the scene on this card we see St. Francis preaching to the birds. This is based on one of the most prevalent images of St. Francis found on holy cards. It illustrates a time when he was observed giving a sermon to a group of birds, much to the amusement of observers. However, the observers were amazed to see the birds fly away afterwards in the formation of a cross to demonstrate their recognition of St. Francis's message.

On the card we can also see St. Francis holding up his hands to display the wounds on his hands known as the *stigmata*. These five wounds that correspond to those of Christ's appeared spontaneously on his body after a vision. St. Francis felt that they were a gift that allowed him to identify with Christ and share his suffering.

St. Francis is the patron of animals, birds, merchants, ecologists, and Italy. His feast day is October 4.

The Tarot Card

All the images in the Tarot come from characters and symbols that can be found in the popular art of the Renaissance. At times, the image in the Tarot is similar to more than one popular icon and one card maker would interpret it differently than another. There are two traditions for the Fool in early decks. One depicts the Fool as a ragged beggar and the other as a jester. In Italian, it is called *il matto*, which means "madman." In French, it is *le mat*, which has no other meaning, and sometimes it is *le fou*, which is synonymous with its English name, the Fool. In early decks, the Fool is almost always unnumbered, even when the other cards in the trumps are numbered. This evidence, combined with its role in the game as a type of wild card, indicates that the Fool is not one of the trumps but something extra. There is also a tradition of considering the Fool as both the lowest and the highest of the trumps. For example, some antique decks—including the Sola Busca—considered the Fool as just the first trump. In these decks the card bears a zero. On the other side, the Fool in the Minchiate is placed after the trumps, and the eighteenth-century Belgian Tarot labels the Fool as number twenty-two.

Tarot Wisdom

The Fool has many seemingly contradictory meanings. It is the most worthless card as well as the most valuable; it is the first and the last. It can represent poverty and illness as well as joy and freedom; a novice, a trusting beginner, and an enlightened master. St. Francis, who was married to poverty and begged in the streets, always joyful, and trusting in God, was one of the most enlightened religious figures in Western history and the ideal saint to play the Fool.

In a reading, pay attention to what the Fool is facing to determine which meaning is being suggested. Are his actions indeed foolish or wisely trusting?

I ▪ St. Nicholas ▪ The Magician

It was the experience of mystery—even if mixed with fear—that engendered religion.

Albert Einstein

The first trump represents a trickster, but in modern decks, this role has been transformed into a magician—a worker of miracles. All saints have been associated with miracles—it is one of the requirements for canonization. With so many saints to choose from it is hard to pick one. However, St. Nicholas is one who is particularly known for miracles that he performed during his lifetime.

The Miracle Worker

Because of his association with Father Christmas or Santa Claus, St. Nicholas is one of the most well-known and best loved of all saints. The historic Nicholas was the Bishop of Myra in Asia Minor in the fourth century. It is said that from the moment of his birth he was destined for the religious life. When he was an infant he stood and sang out praises to God and refused to nurse on fast days. When he inherited his family money, he gave it to the poor.

On one occasion, a citizen of Patara had lost all his money, and because he could not support his three daughters and they could not find husbands because of their poverty, the man was going to give them over to prostitution. When Nicholas heard of this he took a bag of gold, and, under cover of darkness, threw it in the open window of the man's house. Here was a dowry for the eldest girl and she was soon duly married. At intervals, Nicholas did the same for the second and third daughters. This act of charity is represented in the icons of St. Nicholas by the three gold balls that he holds, and which can also be seen in his hands on this card. Pawnbrokers have adopted this image as their symbol and St. Nicholas as their patron.

The three boys in the tub that also appear on this card refer to one of his most startling miracles. During a famine, an innkeeper was able to serve meat to his patrons when no one else was. Nicholas grew suspect and visited the inn to determine where he had attained his meat. In the basement, Nicholas made a gruesome discovery. The innkeeper had killed three children, pickled them in a tub of brine, and was adding their meat to his soup. St. Nicholas raised the boys back to life intact.

On another occasion, Nicholas undertook a voyage at sea. During a storm, waves threatened to overwhelm the ship, but St. Nicholas raised his hand and calmed the sea. Because of this, he is the patron of sailors, as well as children, pawnbrokers, perfumers, and thieves. His feast day is December 6.

The Tarot Card

The original name of the card, *il bagatella,* and its modern Italian name, *il bagatto,* do not mean anything in Italian except the name of this card. The image in the Visconti-Sforza deck shows a man in a broad-brimmed hat sitting at a table with a cake, a glass, and a knife. He has been interpreted as the Carnival king sitting before his meal, or a merchant displaying his wares. However, if we want to understand the popular tradition, we are better off looking at the cards produced from woodblocks, because these are the ones used by most people and reproduced over and over for the playing of the game. One of the oldest woodblock decks can be pieced together from a series of uncut sheets, some of which are in New York's Metropolitan Museum of Art. The Magician in this deck was definitely a street performer/trickster. He has an audience of four people, and is wearing a limp pointed hat without a brim. The only objects that can clearly be identified on his table are a pair of dice. Dice can also be seen on the French Bateleur cards in the deck of Marseilles. These decks also maintain the broad-brimmed hat.

This type of hat would have been considered exotic in the Renaissance. It would be like running into someone in a top hat today. Card historian Ronald Decker makes a connection between this image in the Tarot and Renaissance woodcuts that depict the genius of life bringing new infants into the world, a character that wears a similar hat.[1] This genius is related to the role of psychopomp (the one who leads the soul), one of Hermes/Mercury's roles. In keeping with his role as guide and patron of travelers, Hermes wears a *petasus,* a traveler's hat with a broad brim. This is how he is depicted in ancient sculpture and on vases, and this is how he is often seen in Renaissance portrayals.

The only other place in Renaissance art where one can find a similar gambler/trickster/con man as the one in the Tarot is in astrological illustrations depicting the "children of the planets," the occupations ruled by each planet. As in much of early astrology, the associations are confusing. In one set of pictures, he is associated with the moon and in another with Saturn. But, it is clear in ancient religion that the trickster is under the protection of Hermes, the god of travelers, merchants, alchemists, magicians, liars, and thieves (like St. Nicholas).

In alchemy, Hermes is everywhere: he is the first alchemist, the teacher, the spirit and substance of the Philosopher's Stone. Like Virgil to Dante, he is the alchemist's guide who appears at the beginning of the work. He is also the *prima materia,* the raw material that the alchemist must start with to create the Stone. In texts the prima materia is described as the stone rejected by the builder, something that is thought worthless and trod under foot, but is actually the most valuable thing in the world. The Magician who is first in the order of the trumps and who has the lowest value coincides well with the alchemical Hermes. Also, notice the similarity between this alchemical myth and the myth of the Tarot espoused by Court de Gebelin—the cards are the most valuable book of the ancients, but modern man overlooks it as just a game.

In a classical myth Hermes steals his brother Apollo's cattle, and rather than give them back he trades his invention the lyre for them. The myth goes on to describe a second trade in which Hermes gives Apollo his flute in exchange for the right to be a god of divination. Apollo grants this right on the condition that Hermes' divination will not involve words like *Apollo's oracle.* In the ancient world Hermes presided over divination using signs or tools, primarily dice.

There is evidence that the practice of using dice for divination continued through the Middle Ages into the Renaissance, and that once cards were introduced, cards were substituted for dice in this practice. When we throw two dice, we find that there are twenty-one possible combinations that can come up—the same quantity as the numbered trumps. The *Trionpho della Fortuna,* published in Ferrara in 1526, describes a system of divination using dice. As an alternative to the dice, it provides a wheel with twenty-one astrological figures. In an article written in 1816, Samuel Singer expressed the view that this book influenced *Le Sorti* (1540), one of the first books to describe a system of divination using cards. In *Le Sorti,* nine cards from the suit of coins are used, and the answers are equated to allegorical figures of virtues, follies, and philosophers—images related to the trumps.

Tarot Wisdom

On the most mundane level, this card represents skill, initiations, and beginnings. At a deeper level the Magician of the Tarot of Marseilles points simultaneously to the sky and to the earth, a gesture that communicates Hermes' famous axiom, "As above so below," meaning that the way of Heaven should be manifested on Earth. In keeping with this, the Hermetic texts tell us that it is our purpose, given to us by God, to complete his creation by making the world beautiful. This is what St. Nicholas did by restoring children to life and saving young women from a life of shame. He improved and healed the world and brought Heaven to Earth. This card can help point the way for us to do that in our lives.

II ▪ St. Mary Magdalen ▪ The Papesse

For I am the first and the last.
I am the honored one and the scorned one.
I am the whore and the holy one.
I am the wife and the virgin.

The Thunder, Perfect Mind

This quotation from the beginning of a Gnostic poem was most likely referring to Sophia, the holy wisdom, the female aspect of God. But, as we shall see, it also fits Mary Magdalen with her contradictory and ever-changing role in Christianity. Perhaps this is because she is the embodiment of Sophia.

The First Papesse

The Gnostics hailed Mary Magdalen as the companion of Christ and looked to her above all other apostles. Early Christian writers called her "the Bride of Christ" and "the Apostle to the Apostles." However, her most enduring image is that of a repentant prostitute, a former sinner crying and covering herself in her long, sensual hair. This image, combined with her name, has given us the word *maudlin*. In the development of Christian doctrine, the legend of Mary Magdalen was carefully crafted to discredit Gnostics and to define the role of women in the Church.

The Gospels tell us that Mary Magdalen was chief among the women who followed Jesus and administered to the needs of the disciples. Jesus had cast seven devils out of her. At the crucifixion, she was prominent among a group of women who watched. On the day after the Sabbath, she went to anoint or to observe Christ's body (the Gospels disagree as to whether she was alone or accompanied by two or three other women). Three of the Gospels report that after finding the tomb empty, she became the first person to see Jesus after he had risen. Particularly in the Gospel of St. John, she is the first person to be charged with proclaiming the message of the resurrected Christ.

According to Luke, however, Mary Magdalen returned from the tomb without having met Jesus. After she delivers the news that the tomb is empty to the disciples, Peter decides to investigate. Therefore, in the Gospel of St. Luke, Peter becomes the first to witness the resurrection and is charged with proclaiming the message. Peter became the first pope, and it is on this version of the story that the papal authority rests. Yet, with three accounts awarding her this recognition, it seems that Mary has a claim to the title of "Christ's chosen messenger." She is the ideal figure to serve as the first Papesse.

Mary Magdalen was accorded far greater importance by the Gnostics than she ever was by the orthodox Christians who denied her the status of apostle. The Gnostics chose her as their representative. She embodies the individual visionary experience that the Gnostics valued—the experience that was the basis of their claim of Christ's continued presence. In the Gospel of St. Mary, a Gnostic manuscript attributed to her, it is made clear that she is the beloved of the Savior and the leader of the apostles. In another Gnostic gospel, the Gospel of St. Philip, she is referred to as Christ's *koinonos*, a Greek word usually translated as "companion," but it more accurately means a consort, or spouse. Mary Magdalen, of all the saints, is truly "the Bride of Christ."[2]

In all of the Gnostic literature, it is clear that Mary has received the highest gnosis, or enlightenment. In the *Great Questions of Mary*, an ancient Gnostic text referring to Mary Magdalen, it was claimed that this gnosis was brought on by secret sexual teachings that Christ taught only to her. In the Gospel of St. Mary, she states that Jesus made her into a man, which would mean that by purifying her of the evils of the body, he raised her to an androgynous state. Jesus says in the *Pistis Sophia* ("Faith Wisdom"), another ancient Gnostic text discovered in Egypt in the eighteenth century, that Mary will excel all of his disciples, and he equates her with Sophia, the embodiment of divine wisdom.

As discussed in chapter 2, the ancients believed that as the incarnating soul descended from Heaven toward Earth it passed through the spheres of the seven planets: the sun, moon, Mercury, Venus, Jupiter, Mars, and Saturn. As these seven bodies circled the Earth, each on its own sphere, they formed a ladder between Heaven and Earth. At each of these spheres, the deity, or angel, of the planet clothed the descending soul with certain virtues and vices that became its body. This is the basis of the natal horoscope in astrology.

The Gnostics thought of the soul as a divine essence that entered the physical world in the form of a body. This belief could take a pessimistic form, in which the body was thought of as a prison for the soul, or it could take an optimistic form, in which the body was thought of as the temple of the spirit. The pessimists viewed the contributions of the seven planets as a type of pollution. When a person attained gnosis, they believed that these seven influences were cast out. This is the real meaning of Mark 16:9 which states that Jesus cast seven devils out of Mary. When we understand the hidden meaning, it attests to Mary's enlightenment, but later commentators misread this line as proof of her sinful condition.

The Church officially rejected the validity of the inner visions of the Gnostics and the dominance of Mary Magdalen. They even denied the existence of any female apostles. It is likely that this was the motivation for the creation of her image as a reformed prostitute. Grafting her onto three other women in the Gospels produced this legend. The first was the unnamed adulteress that Jesus saved from punishment. The second was the also unnamed woman described by Luke as a sinner seeking forgiveness who came to Christ at the Pharisee's house, washed his feet with her tears, dried them with her hair, and then anointed them with ointment. The third woman was Mary of Bethany, the sister of Martha and Lazarus, who also anointed Christ's feet with oil and wiped them with her hair. Origen, the great Christian philosopher, used Mary of Bethany as an example of the contemplative life. Thus, the contemplative life was associated with Mary Magdalen as well.

From the second century on, a growing asceticism had steadily gained ground in the Church. There was a strong focus on celibacy, and the image of Mary Magdalen as an ascetic, repentant whore served this purpose. By the sixth century, this legend was firm. It was said that Mary, with Martha and Lazarus, traveled to Provence where she became an evangelist. Later, she retired to a cave where she lived in solitude meditating on her sins. It was claimed that through her great sorrow and repentance she regained her virginity. For women, virginity was considered the most important requirement for sainthood, and Mary's accomplishment made her a major role model for women aspiring to the ideal Christian life. In the Middle Ages, her visionary talents were emphasized, and she became the model and inspiration for all female mystics.

St. Mary Magdalen is the patron of repentant sinners and the contemplative life. Her feast day is July 22.

The Tarot Card

The Papesse is one of most controversial cards in the Tarot. It traditionally depicts a woman in a triple papal tiara sitting on a throne. In her lap, she holds a book—closed in the hand-painted Milanese decks and open in the later French decks. A sixteenth-century deck from Lyon awards her one of the pope's keys. Her purpose in the deck is to serve as a female counterpart or balance to the Pope card. This need for masculine and feminine balance is a major aspect of alchemical and Hermetic philosophy, and exemplifies the Hermetic message that underlies the Tarot. In addition, these early personages in the sequence of trumps are under the domination of Love, the sixth card; therefore, it is natural that they are paired.

The Catholic Church does not ordain women as priests and blocks them from higher offices as well. Only within the convent could a woman attain power by becoming an abbess. From the seventh to the thirteenth centuries, ecclesiastical and teachings orders of nuns flourished. This came to an end in 1545 when the Council of Trent disbanded them in favor of orders that did not educate women. However, they could not eradicate a persistent, popular legend that developed in the ninth century about an educated woman who, disguised as a man, rose through the clergy and then became pope. Her name, Pope Joan, was sometimes associated with the Papesse card, and, although some modern scholars disagree, there is evidence that her legend is based on actual events.

In the thirteenth century, Gugliema of Bohemia, a Gnostic mystic, predicted that in the year 1300 a woman would become pope and initiate a new purified Christianity. Her prediction may have been influenced by the mystical vision of the Cistercian monk, Joachim, who foretold of a coming new age, the Age of the Holy Ghost, which was to contrast the current Age of the Son initiated by Christ. Gugliema's followers believed that this woman was to be the incarnation of the Holy

Ghost, and, although she died in 1281, that she would return in 1300 to crown the first papesse. In 1300, the sect elected Sister Manfreda as the first papesse, and many wealthy Lombard families donated costly vessels for her mass. However, the sect was exterminated by the Inquisition, and Papesse Manfreda was burned at the stake. It is interesting that Papesse Manfreda was a relative of Bianca Visconti-Sforza, the noble who commissioned the painting of one of the oldest existing Tarot decks.

In Renaissance art, the figure of a woman with a triple tiara is sometimes used as an allegorical figure representing the papacy as something separate from the pope. An orthodox interpretation of this card may be that the pope's own office is his wife. However, that is not in keeping with the nature of this first act of the trumps, which depicts the triumph of Cupid. In *The Dream of Poliphilo,* a mystical fiction work written in 1467 and noted for its beautiful dreamlike illustrations, we can find the figure of a woman who, like the Papesse, is sitting on a throne and wearing a triple-layered crown and a long robe. Here she represents the priestess of Venus and can be seen counseling Poliphilo and his love, Polia. That the Papesse represents the priestess of Venus, the head of a Pagan religion that was triumphed over by the religion of the pope, is more in keeping with the first act in this allegory.

Tarot Wisdom

On the card, Mary Magdalen stands in front of Christ's empty tomb after witnessing his resurrection. She is framed in the portal as the guardian of mystery. On the pilasters can be seen the first and last letters of the Greek alphabet, alpha and omega. Together these form a symbol for Christ as the beginning and the end, the one whose death is the beginning of life, who is beyond opposites and one with the infinite. Mary, as his female counterpart, also embodies this mystery.

This card represents mystery, which can be described as an inner, esoteric religious experience, and stands in contrast to outer, exoteric religion symbolized by the Pope. In modern usage, the word *mystery* means a puzzle, something to be explained, but in the original meaning mystery is something that can only be experienced, that cannot be explained. It is the origin of the word *mystical.* Symbolically it is linked to the feminine sex whose organs of reproduction are hidden, and the exoteric is linked to the masculine whose sexuality is external. Therefore, it is natural that the Tarot would choose a feminine figure, the Papesse, to symbolize mystery and a masculine figure, the Pope, for the exoteric.

On a more mundane level, Mary Magdalen stands for intuition, knowledge that is hidden, or knowledge that cannot be expressed in words.

III ▪ St. Helena ▪ The Empress

The world would have peace if the men of politics would only follow the Gospels.

St. Birgitta of Sweden

The quotation above from St. Birgitta (1303–1373), who was the daughter of a governor in Sweden, expresses a sentiment that St. Helena, who was surrounded by the powerful men who ruled the Roman Empire, might well have identified with.

The Empress of Rome

St. Helena was a native of Bithynia, a poor innkeeper's daughter who married the then Roman general Constantius I in about 270. Their son, Constantine, was born soon after, and in 293 Constantius was made caesar, or junior emperor. However, for political reasons he divorced Helena to marry the co-Emperor Maximian's stepdaughter. Her son, Constantine, became emperor in 312 after the fateful victory at Milvian Bridge, and Helena was named augusta, or empress.

As empress, Helena converted to Christianity and performed many acts of charity, including building churches in Rome and in the Holy Land, and using the imperial treasure to aid the poor. In 362, she made a pilgrimage to the Holy Land. Because Golgotha and the Holy Sepulchre had been laid bare by the removal of the temple of Venus's terrace that had covered them, Helena went there hoping to find the remains of the true cross. One night in a dream Christ came to her and showed her where to look. The next day she uncovered the cross, Christ's coat, and the three nails of the crucifixion.

St. Helena is the patron of divorced people, converts, and empresses. Her feast day is August 18.

The Tarot Card

In all early decks, the Empress card is a clear reference to the wife of the Holy Roman Emperor (although Constantine, it seems, attached this status more to his mother than to his wife). After the fall of the Roman Empire in the West, the Catholic Church began to view itself as a continuation of the empire in spiritual form as it attempted to unite the West into one religious body instead of a political body. With the rise of the powerful monarch Charlemagne, the Church saw a way to reclaim the political aspect of its empire, and in 800 Charlemagne was crowned by the pope as "Emperor of the Romans." Although at times this Holy Roman Empire was more of a symbol than a reality, it was strengthened by Otto the Great in 936 and existed in various forms for approximately one thousand years. The city-states of northern Italy where the Tarot originated were part of the empire from the time of Charlemagne.

The Empress sits on a throne. Most often she is depicted holding a shield or orb in one hand and a scepter in the other. The shield typically bears an eagle as the heraldic emblem of the Holy Roman Empire. The eagle, a symbol of Zeus, was the emblem of the Roman legions and in the Middle Ages became the symbol of Rome. When Charlemagne became emperor, he combined the Roman eagle, which faces left, with the German eagle, which faces right, into one two-headed eagle facing in both directions. This two-headed eagle became the coat of arms of all the emperors. We can see this emblem in art from the Renaissance, such as Dürer's woodcuts depicting the Emperor Maximilian. In early printed cards, we can see this two-headed eagle on the Empress and Emperor cards. However, in the hand-painted Milanese decks, the Tarot of Marseilles, and many of the decks based on the latter we find a single-headed eagle on each card. The Visconti-Sforza gives the Roman eagle (facing left) to the Empress and the German eagle to the Emperor, and the deck of Marseilles does the opposite.

There is a Greek myth in which Zeus sets two eagles free to fly in opposite directions until they meet face-to-face in the sacred center of the world. The place where they met was Delphi, and the Greeks erected a stone, called the *omphalos,* to mark that spot. As was mentioned in chapter 3, the most ancient way of depicting the sacred center was to create an image of two animals face-to-face. In the Renaissance, the alchemists made use of this myth as a symbol of their quest for gnosis; it is illustrated in the famous alchemical text *Atalanta Fugiens.* The eagles facing in opposite directions on the Empress and Emperor cards at the beginning of the Tarot trumps may be a reference to this mystical quest. Especially when we consider that their goal, the sacred center, is illustrated on the last trump.

Tarot Wisdom

In liturgical art, as on this Tarot card, Helena is depicted as an empress holding the true cross. She is sumptuously dressed. She is on the shore of a foreign land, but she has followed her vision and what she sought was miraculously delivered. The Empress represents the feminine principle, the principle that is attractive and attracts what it desires.

IV ▪ ST. CONSTANTINE ▪ THE EMPEROR

In hoc signo vinces. *("In this sign thou shalt conquer.")*

The motto of Constantine

The Latin motto stated above was originally seen by Constantine in a vision. The sign that it is referring to is the vision of the cross with the symbol of Christ in the center.

The First Christian Emperor

St. Constantine is the son of the Junior Emperor Constantius and St. Helena. He is often called the Thirteenth Apostle in the East. Constantine was raised on the court of co-Emperor Diocletian. When his father died in 306, Constantine was declared junior emperor in York, England, by the local legions under his command. At first he was satisfied with his position and avoided the struggles for power that characterized the empire at that time, but in 312 he was drawn into a struggle with his brother-in-law Maxentius at Milvian Bridge.

As the battle neared, Constantine assessed his chances and feared that he would meet defeat, but on the eve before the battle, he saw a vision that changed his fate and that of the Western world. In the sun, he saw a cross of light with the monogram of Christ in the center and the words "In this sign thou shalt conquer." Constantine won the battle and all of the conflicts that followed. He became the sole ruler of the empire. He adopted the insignia of his vision, the *chi-rho* (a monogram of Christ's name formed by its first two letters in Greek), in the center of a cross as his labarum, his military standard. A purple banner was later added to the labarum that was emblazoned with the monogram from his vision.

For better or worse, St. Constantine was the most dominating figure of his lifetime; he towered over his contemporaries, including Pope Sylvester I. St. Constantine ended the persecution of Christians. He presided over the Council of Nicaea, gave extensive grants of land and property to the Church, renamed the city of Byzantium Constantinople and made it his new capital, and undertook a long-sighted program of Christianization for the whole of the Roman Empire. While he was baptized a Christian only on his deathbed, he most likely considered himself a Christian since the time of his vision.

St. Constantine is venerated by the Eastern Orthodox Christians. It is easy to make a comparison between his cult and those of the warrior heroes of antiquity. As a saint, he does not always measure up to a modern standard of enlightened morality. For example, it is said that because of a lying accusation from his wife, Fausta, he hastily put his son to death. Later, he had his wife boiled alive. Many historians debate the benefits of his influence on Christianity. Making the Church a rich powerful institution helped to separate it from the needs of the people and it certainly marked the beginning of the end for most Gnostics. However, in many ways, he was a model of tolerance, passing laws that protected Pagans and Christians alike. His religious observances were a synthesis of beliefs and his soldiers were given a public prayer that was nonspecific and would be tolerable to any religion. It was Constantine's sons who, after his death, enacted laws to persecute Pagans and heretics and set precedence for the Inquisition.

St. Constantine is the patron of emperors. His feast day is May 21.

The Tarot Card

The design of this card has changed very little through the centuries. The Holy Roman Emperor sits on his throne—in the French decks in profile—holding a scepter and accompanied by the heraldic eagle. As explained in the discussion of the Empress card above, his eagle is two-headed, but this was not always the case in the Tarot. Sometimes his eagle may appear on his hat or become a sculptural side to his throne. In some nineteenth-century decks his heraldic device becomes a cross.

Tarot Wisdom

St. Constantine stands on the card in his imperial robe holding his labarum. In front is the sun, the symbol of his vision. The sun is rising, as Constantine represents the dawn of a new era. The Emperor can represent a powerful person or our own power and intelligence. He orders his world and dictates changes. He makes the insights of the Empress into law.

V ▪ St. Peter ▪ The Pope

And I say also unto thee, that thou art Peter, and upon this rock I will build my church: and the gates of hell shall not prevail against it.

And I will give unto thee the keys of the kingdom of heaven: and whatsoever thou shalt bind on earth shall be bound in heaven; and whatsoever thou shalt loose on earth shall be loosed in heaven.

Matthew 16:18–19

With these words spoken by Christ at the Last Supper, Peter became the first pope.

The First Pope

At birth, his name was Simon; Jesus changed his name to Peter or Cephas, which means "rock." St. Peter became the first pope, the "Prince of the Apostles," and cofounder, with St. Paul, of the See of Rome. Peter was a fisherman with his brother Andrew on Lake Genesareth by the Sea of Galilee. It was Andrew who introduced him to Jesus. Jesus came to the lake where they were fishing and said he was to be a "fisher of men" (Matthew 4:19). St. Peter was the first of the apostles to perform miracles in the name of the Lord, and was instrumental in bringing the gospel to the Gentiles, thereby helping the Church to become universal. His missionary efforts led him to Antioch, Corinth, and eventually Rome.

At times, Peter displayed human weaknesses. When Jesus was arrested, he attempted to defend Jesus by cutting off the right ear of a slave of the high priest Malchus. Later, he denied Christ three times as his master had predicted. Peter then "went out and began to weep bitterly" (Luke 22:62). Yet, Christ valued Peter as the head of the apostles (although Gnostics would say that Christ awarded Mary Magdalen that role), and charged him with the task of building his Church. As declared in the quotation above (Matthew 16:18–19), he was given the keys to Heaven, one of gold and one of silver, and they can be seen in his left hand on this card.

Peter was martyred in Rome under the reign of Nero. He was crucified on the Vatican Hill upside down because he declared himself unworthy to die in the same manner as his Lord (which makes him a candidate for the Hanged Man card as well); he was then buried on Vatican Hill. His relics are now enshrined under the high altar of St. Peter's and all popes look to him as their predecessor, the first pope.

At the time Peter was called by Jesus, he was married to a woman named Perpetua. Christ deliberately chose him to head the Church knowing that he was married. Peter left his wife to be with Jesus for about three years, but on his master's death, he returned to her. According to traditional belief, Peter brought Perpetua with him to Rome when he set up the Roman See, and there she preached and baptized converts. Therefore, Perpetua can also be considered the first papesse.

St. Peter is the patron of the Church and of popes. And while his chief feast day is June 29, he is also honored on February 22 and November 18.

The Tarot Card

When the Tarot was first created, the Protestant Reformation had not yet occurred, and with no one to challenge him, the pope was considered the highest of the temporal rulers, the highest worldly authority. After all, he had the power to crown the emperor and represented God's authority on Earth. In one of the oldest decks painted for the Visconti-Sforza family, the rulers of Milan, the Pope is a white-bearded man sitting on a throne wearing a triple crown, holding a cross in his left hand, and making the sign of benediction with his right. In later decks his cross becomes triple, two columns are added to his throne, and two petitioners are set before him with their backs to us. In some decks he is holding St. Peter's keys or has them in a heraldic device.

After the Reformation, the Church of Rome became less accepting of the Pope and Papesse cards, and we sometimes find other characters being substituted for them. In the Minchiate, the Papesse was removed and the Pope became the Eastern Emperor. In the Swiss deck, they became Juno and Jupiter, and in the Flemish deck, they were replaced by the Spanish Captain and Bacchus. A. E. Waite changed their names to the High Priestess and the Hierophant.

Tarot Wisdom

St. Peter sits on his throne which is drawn from the one his statue sits on in the Vatican. He holds the keys to Heaven in his left hand and gives the sign of benediction with his right. He is the earthly spokesman for God, receiving his inspiration through the light from above.

The Pope represents the exoteric aspects of religion verses the esoteric represented by the Papesse. He is religion for the masses, the power that makes moral judgments. The Pope determines what is right and what is wrong. Pay attention to which way he is facing.

VI ▪ St. Valentine and The Lovers

Therefore once for all this short command is given to you: Love and do what you will. If you keep silent, keep silent by love; if you speak, speak by love; if you correct, correct by love; if you pardon, pardon by love: let love be rooted in you, and from the root nothing but good can grow.

Saint Augustine of Hippo

The first line of this quotation from St. Augustine expressing the essence of unconditional love will be familiar to many students of the occult. It seems that it may have influenced the infamous occult writer Aleister Crowley.

The Patron of Lovers

There is some confusion as to which St. Valentine we celebrate on the holiday named after him on February 14. There are two Valentines, both venerated on the same day. One was a Roman priest martyred in 269 and the other a bishop of Terni martyred several years earlier. Some have even suggested that the holiday is named after the Gnostic leader Valentinus who was noted for his sanctification of sexual practices. The weight of opinion, however, falls on Valentine the priest.

The February 14 holiday is most likely a continuation of the Roman Lupercalia, a Roman holiday held in honor of Juno in mid-February. On the eve of Lupercalia, young men would draw the name of a suitable mate from a jar and agree to remain faithful to her for a year. It is believed that our modern holiday is a Christianization of this practice.

According to the legend, Valentine was a priest in Rome under the reign of Emperor Claudius II. The emperor had ordered that all soldiers should remain unmarried so that they would not create any attachments that would interfere with their duties—especially when they were ordered to leave for war. Valentine defied the emperor and secretly married the soldiers and their brides. He was eventually arrested and sent to prison to await his execution. While in prison he fell in love with the blind daughter of the jailer, and through his faith, he miraculously restored her vision. When he was led away to his death, he signed his farewell message to her "from your Valentine."

St. Valentine is the patron of lovers. His feast day is February 14.

The Tarot Card

The sixth trump in the Tarot represents the triumph of love—the triumph of Cupid—over all the worldly couples that come before it. In early decks, we can find two different traditions reflected in the illustrations on this card. Originally in the Italian decks, this card was called simply "Love" and depicted a man and woman with Cupid above them. These images were based on Renaissance betrothal portraits and represent a betrothal or a marriage—similar to what we find on Valentine cards today. In the hand-painted Gringonneur deck (another early Italian deck), the figures are multiplied with three couples and two Cupids.

In France, the tradition changed. The title was changed to "The Lovers" and a third figure was added. At first, the third figure was possibly a priest performing the marriage of the lovers, but over time he transformed into a second woman representing an alternative choice for the central man. Now the theme became choice or temptation. The man had to choose between study or virtue as represented by a woman sometimes crowned with a laurel wreath, and sensuality or vice as represented by a woman sometimes crowned with flowers. This is a theme that can be traced to teachings of Pythagoras and is in keeping with the allegory of the trumps in which the virtues trump Cupid.

Tarot Wisdom

St. Valentine plays the part of Cupid hovering over the lovers in this card, just as his spirit presides over Valentine's Day. This card represents love in all its aspects. If we follow its lead, love in any form can deliver us to the highest good. From sexual attraction to unconditional love, they form one continuum. This is the message of Plato's *Symposium* and Dante's *Divine Comedy* and it is the message of the Tarot.

VII ▪ St. Christopher ▪ The Chariot

When a man is purged of all attachments to things, the judgement is left clear as the sky when the mists have disappeared. His joy is not dependent on the creatures, for while his heart is set on none of them he possesses them all.

St. John of the Cross

Although St. Christopher has been removed from the calendar and he is not likely to have been an actual person, his story seems crafted to illustrate the sentiment expressed above. His name means "Christ-bearer," a reference to his story. Because he carried Christ, he became the patron of travelers and the best saint to play the part of the Chariot in the *Tarot of the Saints*.

The Patron of Travelers

According to legend, St. Christopher was a large, homely man of great physical strength who declared that he wanted to work for the greatest king on earth. At first he sought out the devil, but realizing that the devil was fearful of Christ, Christopher left him to search for this greater master. A holy hermit instructed Christopher that to achieve his desire he should live by the edge of a certain deep and treacherous river and help travelers to cross it. Christopher heeded his advice and helped many travelers.

One stormy night when the river was swollen and the undercurrent sharp, a child came to cross the river. To see the child safely across, Christopher put him on his back and waded into the current. As he progressed, his task became harder. With every step, the child grew heavier and the river more forceful, but St. Christopher persevered and eventually reached the other side. Once they were safely on shore, the child revealed himself to be Jesus, the creator of the world, and it was the weight of his creation that Christopher had born. As proof of his identity, Christ instructed Christopher to plant his staff in the ground. The next morning Christopher found that it had turned into a tree and was bearing fruit.

After this miracle, Christopher had himself baptized and became a wandering preacher. Eventually he was imprisoned because of his faith. The king used both the allure of prostitutes (the triumph of Cupid) and the pain of torture (the Hanged Man) to get Christopher to abandon Christianity, but both methods were unsuccessful. Finally, Christopher was beheaded. As St. Christopher died, he prayed that in the future he would be able to save the faithful from fire, storm, and disaster.

The early icons of St. Christopher show him with a dog's head. His image is similar to the Hellenistic Egyptian god Hermanubis, a jackal-headed synthesis of the Egyptian god Anubis with the Greek god Hermes. This god was a psychopomp—the ultimate patron of travelers—

who led the soul in the afterlife and presided over its resurrection. This aspect is symbolized in St. Christopher's story by the rebirth of his staff. To explain his strange appearance, a story was crafted in which he asked the Lord to made him as ugly as a dog to escape the attentions of females. In the Middle Ages, it was believed that once an individual had seen an image of St. Christopher, he or she would be protected from disaster and sudden death for the rest of the day.

St. Christopher is the patron of travelers, pilgrims, drivers, and motorists. Before he was removed from the calendar, his feast day was July 25.

The Tarot Card

The Chariot is a triumphal car often found in allegorical triumphs in Renaissance art. In the Italian decks it was called *Il Carro* ("The Chariot"), or sometimes *Il Carro Triumphale* ("The Triumphal Chariot"). This card provides further evidence that the trumps are an allegorical parade. The hand-painted Italian decks, except for the Gringonneur, depict a chariot in profile with a female driver; most often, the two horses are winged. This image relates to Laura, the triumph of virtue, in Petrarch's *I Trionphi* (chapter 2). On a deeper level it also relates to the image of the soul as a female charioteer with winged steeds created by Plato in *Phaedrus*. In Plato's myth, the feathers on the horses represent virtue, and through unvirtuous behavior they are lost, causing the chariot to descend.

In the Gringonneur and in printed decks (except for Minchiates which has a nude female charioteer), the Chariot is facing the viewer and the driver is male. This figure is often armored like a warrior prince and usually equated with Mars or Sol in his chariot. Here again the image represents discipline and virtue trumping Cupid.

Tarot Wisdom

On the card, the infant Jesus rides St. Christopher as his chariot. St. Christopher is wading safely to shore using his living staff for support. This card represents travel, safety, protection, and discipline.

VIII ▪ St. Michael ▪ Justice

Mercy and truth are met together; righteousness and peace have kissed each other.

Psalm 25:10

According to traditional belief, St. Michael authored the psalm the above quotation is taken from. The quotation makes it clear that justice is an instrument of peace and order, not revenge. Like the Egyptian god Thoth, Michael weighs the souls of the dead to determine their final destination; he determines what is just. He is one of the seven archangels, who can be equated to the seven virtues. Depicted in art with the scales in his hand, he is the perfect saint to play the part of Justice in the Tarot.

The Author of the Law

St. Michael is one of the three angels mentioned by name in Holy Scripture. The name *Michael* signifies "who is like God." He is called "Chief of the Order of Virtues," "Chief of the Seven Archangels," and "Prince of the Angels." He has been especially honored and invoked as patron and protector by the Church from the time of the apostles. In Phygia he replaced the god of the thermal waters, in Gaul he took the place of Mercury, and in Germany, Wotan. Constantine dedicated a church to him and believed he was responsible for the emperor's victories. Everywhere he is venerated as the protector of Christians.

The image of Michael on his icons—and on the Tarot card—is based on his role in the final battle with Satan described in Revelation 12:7–8: "Michael and his angels fought against the dragon; and the dragon fought and his angels, and prevailed not; neither was their place found any more in Heaven."

After Satan is defeated, Michael casts him into a fiery pit for a thousand years. As a warrior, he is depicted in armor brandishing a sword, but he also carries the scales of judgment. As psychopomp, after weighing the souls of the dead, he leads the righteous to their reward in Heaven. St. Michael not only protects but rescues souls from Hell.

St. Michael is the patron of grocers, mariners, paratroopers, police, the sick, and the Church. His feast day is September 29.

The Tarot Card

Justice is the first of the four cardinal virtues to appear in the Marseilles order of the trumps (A. E. Waite switched the placement of Strength and Justice without historical precedence but for the purpose of his astrological associations). Only three of the four virtues are depicted in the Tarot. They are cardinal because they relate to the fourfold limits of time and space. For more information on this see chapter 2 and the discussion of the Tarot card under St. Catherine.

The image of Justice that appears in the Tarot—a woman holding a sword in one hand and scales in the other—is one that is still familiar in modern culture. However, unlike the modern image, the Tarot's Justice is not blind. The blindfold was not attributed to her until the sixteenth century and still did not usually appear in the Tarot. In the early Renaissance the blindfold would have been interpreted as ignorance—an undesirable quality for Justice. Her image is based on the Greek goddess Themis, who was Zeus's first or second wife and who stood at his side even after he married Hera. Like Michael, Themis represents justice as a force of good in the universe. She is divine law personified. Themis forsook the Earth after the golden age, but her daughter Dike (also called Asteraea), who represents earthly justice, stayed on until the Bronze Age. It is Dike who entered the zodiac as Virgo with her scales next to her in Libra.

Tarot Wisdom

St. Michael stands on the dragon—Satan—and subdues him but does not destroy him. In his left hand he holds the scales, his tool for finding truth. In his right hand he holds his weapon the sword. Where his scales must be used impartially and without prejudice to do their job, the use of the sword is a responsibility that must be tempered with mercy. St. Michael represents truth, fairness, protection, and dealings with the law.

IX ▪ St. Anthony of Egypt ▪ The Hermit

Many have gone through great feats of self-mortification and endured much labor and sweat for the sake of God; but their self-will, lack of good judgment, and the fact that they do not deem it necessary to seek salutary advice from their brethren, make these labors useless and vain.

St. Mark the Ascetic

As the above quotation states, for asceticism to deliver us from egotism it must not be an egotistical act in itself. St. Anthony of Egypt is one of the first Christian ascetics and a model for the wandering holy men of the Middle Ages. Therefore, he is also the model for the holy hermit in the Tarot.

The Hermit

When Anthony was young, he listened as the following passage, Matthew 19:21, was read in church one day: "If you wish to be perfect, go, sell your possessions, and give the money to the poor, and you will have treasure in heaven; then come, follow me." Right then, Anthony walked out the door and gave away all his property except what he and his sister needed to live on. Later, still not content that he had done enough, he gave away everything else, entrusted his sister to a convent, and went outside the village to live a life of praying, fasting, and manual labor.

Anthony's reputation for holiness grew and people sought him out to talk to him and to be healed by him. He kept moving further out of town until, finally, he moved into the desert. No one had braved the desert before. He lived sealed in a room for twenty years while his friends provided bread. Eventually, people came and broke down his door to be with him. Anthony was not angered by this but calmly emerged and healed them with his words. Some of the people stayed to learn from him and formed the first Christian monastic community, one in which all of the monks lived separately and came together only for worship and to hear Anthony speak.

Artists love to depict the temptations that the devil tormented St. Anthony with while he was alone in his retreat. Their creations embody all the lusts and fears that assaulted him, but which he patiently overcame. Anthony always said that the key to the ascetic life was perseverance. To most people perserverance means not giving up, but to Anthony perseverance meant beginning each day with renewed zeal and commitment. He lived as if every day of his life was the first day. On the day when he heard the words of Matthew, he responded by giving up his property, but he did not stop there. On the next day, he asked himself what else he could do, how else could he help others, and what could he do to be closer to God. Although he only ate bread and ate only once a day, he lived to the age of 105.

In Anthony's icon, as on this Tarot card, he is accompanied by a pig which symbolized the lust that he overcame, and he is ringing a bell to drive away evil. His staff is shaped like a tau cross (named after the Greek letter equivalent to a *T*). His followers, called the Order of Hospitallers, raised pigs, wore similar hoods, and carried bells.

St. Anthony is the patron of hermits, monks, domestic animals, and basket makers. His feast day is January 27.

The Tarot Card

The earliest Italian cards depict the Hermit as an old man on crutches or holding an hourglass. There is one Italian printed card depicting the more familiar holy hermit holding a lantern and a staff, and this is the image we find in the French cards and their offshoots. The old man is an image of time, often depicted in Renaissance art and still used in modern New Year's Eve celebrations. That Time would appear in the second section of the trumps is in keeping with the theme presented by the other cards in this section. Transforming the image into a wandering mendicant, a character in Christian culture that directly evolved from the example set by St. Anthony, illustrates a spiritual path that can lead out of the trap of time—a sacred meditation that will lead us to the last section of the Tarot.

Tarot Wisdom

St. Anthony stands on the card with his pig at his side which represents desire or his hopes, and holds his bell which represents protection from evil or his fears. St. Anthony stands between his hopes and fears. Through meditation, he has found the middle ground of peace, beyond hope and fear, that allows him (and us) to experience gnosis.

At its most mundane level, this card can simply express the need or desire to be alone. Solitude can be a welcome rest or an enforced loneliness.

X ▪ St. Catherine ▪ Wheel of Fortune

To every thing there is a season, and a time to every purpose under the heaven:

A time to be born, and a time to die; A time to plant, and a time to pluck up that which is planted;

A time to kill, and a time to heal; A time to break down, and a time to build up;

A time to weep, and a time to laugh; A time to mourn, and a time to dance; . . .

Ecclesiastes 3:1–4

St. Catherine is one of the most popular saints of legend, despite the fact that her legend is probably not based on an actual, historic person. In the Middle Ages, she was second only to Mary in public adoration. We can see in her story an idealized model for all Christian nuns, and it contains many archetypal symbols that appealed to medieval artists.

The Patron of the Wheel

Catherine was said to be a princess and the most beautiful young woman in her time. Fourth-century Alexandria, where she lived, was a center of philosophy and learning, and Catherine studied until she had mastered every field of knowledge. Naturally, when it was time for her to marry she sought a husband who was as handsome and learned as her, but these conditions were not easy to meet.

One day Ananias, a Christian hermit, (as discussed in the story of St. Anthony, Alexandria and other areas in Egypt were the birthplace of this Christian ascetic practice) told her that if she prayed to the Virgin Mary, a husband would be delivered to her. She did as he asked. That night the Virgin came to her in a dream, and introduced her to Jesus. But when the Virgin asked her son if he wanted Catherine for a bride, he complained that she was too ugly. Catherine was distraught when she awoke. She went to the hermit to ask for help, and he explained that Jesus was not referring to a lack of physical beauty, but instead to the lack of beauty in her soul. To remedy her spiritual "ugliness," the hermit baptized her and instructed her in Christianity. The next time Jesus appeared in her dream he found her perfectly beautiful, and placed a gold ring on her finger. When she awoke, she found that the ring was still there. This is called "the mystical marriage of St. Catherine," and through this miracle, she was considered the "Bride of Christ."

At the age of eighteen, Catherine went to Emperor Maximinus to denounce him for his persecution of Christians. The emperor, finding himself unable to refute her arguments, summoned fifty scholars to aid him, but Catherine succeeded in converting all of them to Christianity. Only the emperor seemed immune to her logic. He was not, however, immune to her beauty. He lusted after her with determination, only to find all of his propositions declined. The enraged Maximinus threw Catherine in prison, and had the fifty scholars burned alive.

In prison, Catherine converted her jailers and the empress, who had come to visit her. Once again, the emperor responded by falling into a murderous rage. He executed all of the converts, including his wife. Then he had the audacity to propose to Catherine. She, of course, was already married to a husband more wise and powerful than Maximinus, and his monstrous behavior did not help to win her affection.

The emperor determined that if he could not have Catherine, he would have her killed. For this purpose, he ordered the construction of a machine that consisted of four great, spiked wheels that turned in alternating directions. Catherine was placed in this machine to be ripped apart, but lightning struck instead and shattered the wheels. Undaunted, the emperor then had her beheaded. From her severed head milk flowed instead of blood. Her body was born by angels to Mount Sinai where a monastery was built in her honor. Her relics were later discovered on this spot, and her bones constantly exuded a healing unguent.

Milk flowing from a wound instead of blood became a constant in the legends of saints. This symbol can be compared to the alchemical image called the "Siren of the Philosophers," a mermaid who emits blood from her right breast and milk from her left. Red and white are the masculine and feminine opposites in alchemy, but in blood and milk, the colors take on the added meaning of the power of death and life. The siren, the source of these fluids, can be seen as a continuation of the mother goddess archetype in Christian Europe. By spouting milk, the nurturing fluid of life, instead of blood, St. Catherine's martyrdom becomes a triumph over death. Her death nurtures life just as her bones heal with their unguent. She becomes one with the mother goddess, and is truly the bride or female counterpart of God.

St. Catherine's name is derived from the Greek *Catharina,* which means "pure." Her association with the archetype of the wheel no doubt accounts for her immense popularity. It enabled her to become a Christian version of Fortuna, the Roman goddess of fate. It is this association that also earns her a place in this Tarot.

St. Catherine is the patron of scholars and philosophers, and because she is from fourth-century Alexandria, it may be assumed that she is the patron of Hermeticism and Neoplatonic philosophy, the mystical philosophies that stem from there and were accepted by the medieval and Renaissance Church. Because of her association with the wheel, she is the patron of all occupations that relate to wheels. Her feast day is November 25.

The Tarot Card

The Wheel of Fortune earns its central position in the sequence of Tarot trumps because its message underlies the entire allegory. Fortune's wheel, although it was named after the Roman goddess of fate, Fortuna, was a popular image throughout the Middle Ages and the Renaissance. The Church found it useful because it could attach a moralistic message to it.

The mystical poet and scholar Robert Graves points out that the Romans derived the name of the goddess Fortuna from the Etruscan goddess, Vortumna, whose name means "she who turns the wheel of the year."[2] The wheel of the year refers to the zodiac, the path that the sun follows as it waxes, wanes, and is reborn to a new year. Like moon gods before him, the sun god was a hero guided by Fate on his journey. Fate was his mother, his lover, and his death leading to rebirth. This triple aspect of Fate was often personified as three separate goddesses. The Greeks called them Clotho, Lachesis, and Atropos. We can find the same archetypes in the goddesses that the Romans named Fortuna Primigenia, Bona Fortuna, and Mala Fortuna, three of the many aspects of the goddess of fortune.

The wheel of the year is divided into four cardinal points that corresponded to the journey of the sun. As explained in chapter 2, the classical world used the word *cardinalis* to refer to the principal turning points on the wheel of the year, and to the four directions and the four winds. In Medieval Latin, *cardinalis* came to mean "chief" or "principal." It was used to refer to prominent bishops, particularly the ones that elected the pope. St. Ambrose used this term to refer to the four chief moral virtues that had been expounded on by Plato and Aristotle: temperance, justice, fortitude, and prudence. These were called the cardinal virtues and later were added to the three theological or Christian virtues—faith, hope, and charity—to create the mystical seven.

On the earliest surviving Wheel of Fortune card painted for the Visconti-Sforza family circa 1445, Fortuna stands in the center of her wheel surrounded by four male figures. These figures can be seen as a satirical, microcosmic version of the sun's cardinal quest. The man on the left climbs the wheel. He is sprouting ass's ears, and a ribbon issuing from his mouth can be translated as "I will reign." On top of the wheel a man sits holding a mace and an orb. He is crowned with full-grown ass's ears and declares, "I do reign." Descending the wheel headfirst, a man with an ass's tail but no ears bemoans, "I have reigned." Finally, at the bottom, a crawling man simply says, "I am without reign." The message of this allegory seems identical to that of the Buddhist wheel of life, which depicts the fate of the unenlightened as an endless cycle of deaths and rebirths. In the center of the Buddhist wheel, there are three foolish creatures chasing one another's tails. Similarly, the Tarot of Marseilles depicts three foolish creatures following each other around a wheel on this card. In the Christian world, only heretics could have seen a message about reincarnation; to the Church it depicted the folly of striving for worldly gains.

The cards that surround the Wheel of Fortune in the traditional Tarot reiterate its theme. The Chariot represents youthful upward striving. The Hermit represents the attainment of age and wisdom. The Hanged Man is literally headed down, and Death is certainly without reign. Among them, we find three of the four cardinal virtues: justice, fortitude, and temperance. Tarot scholars have been puzzled by the absence of the fourth cardinal virtue prudence, or wisdom. It is likely that the Wheel of Fortune itself, with its moralistic perspective, represents prudence, or that prudence was left out because the other three virtues correspond to the triple aspects of Fate. Fortitude is Fortuna Primigenia, temperance is Bona Fortuna, and justice is Mala Fortuna.

Tarot Wisdom

On this card, St. Catherine is seen in her archetypal role with the wheel of fate and holding her martyr's palm. On the wheel, waxing and waning symbols mark the solstices and the equinoxes. In the corners, the four winds blow from the cardinal directions. Their names are Boreas, the north wind; Euros, the east wind; Notos, the south wind; and Zephyros, the west wind.

St. Catherine's message is one of change and patience. All things change, and, as her quotation states, there is a time for every purpose. If times are good then we should save for the lean times. If times are lean then they will be better in the future. The fact that all things change most often works in our favor; stagnation would be its opposite. Therefore, this card can be viewed as an omen of good fortune.

XI ▪ St. Jerome ▪ Strength

Give me strength to raise my head to a level with the saint's heels.

St. Jerome

This quotation from St. Jerome suggests great humility. The facts of his life tell us that humility was not something that came easily to him. He was often critical and self-righteous, and people sometimes found him offensive. Yet, it is said that he was loved by a lion.

Who Tamed the Lion

St. Jerome was born in 340 to a wealthy family in Dalmata. His parents furnished him with a quality education and he studied Latin and Greek literature. Jerome was baptized when he was eighteen by Pope Liberius. As an ambitious and a disciplined worker, Jerome began building a library that became one of the most famous in the world by copying most of the books himself. He continued this practice while living as a hermit in Palestine and Egypt and learning Hebrew and other languages to facilitate his work. Throughout his life, Jerome tried to reconcile his love of the classics of Pagan literature with his Christian beliefs. Like St. Augustine, he tried to make a synthesis of the two but he was not always successful and the struggle caused him much suffering.

In 382, Jerome was called to Rome by Pope Damasus, and under his direction St. Jerome copied the Bible into Latin. His translation, called the *Vulgate,* remains the most influential piece of literature produced in the fourth century. On the death of Pope Damasus who was his supporter and protector, Jerome decided to return to the East, and eventually settled in Bethlehem with a small community he had formed.

According to legend, Jerome made friends with a lion by removing a thorn from its paw (like the story of Androcles). The lion stayed with him and guarded the monastery, but one day the monastery donkey disappeared. Thinking that the lion ate the donkey, all the monks condemned him except Jerome. He alone acted with patience and trust, realizing that there was no conclusive proof that the lion was guilty. Eventually the lion found the donkey and brought him home along with camels belonging to the thieves.

St. Jerome is a "Doctor of the Church" and the patron of librarians and scholars. His feast day is September 30.

The Tarot Card

In the French decks this card is titled *La Force,* and in Italian, it is called *La Fortezza;* both names refer to the virtue fortitude or strength.

Although the virtues epitomize the qualities of often masculine ancient heroes, the virtue itself is usually depicted in art as female. There are two distinct modes of depicting strength in the Tarot, and both are references to ancient strongmen.

On this card in the Tarot of Marseilles and its offshoots we find a woman gently subduing a lion—a reference to Hercules and the Nemean Lion, the first of his twelve labors, or possibly to Samson. This image, which sometimes has the woman astride the lion, can also be compared to the Greek goddess Rhea who rides a lion. A woman riding a lion was popularized in the Renaissance by an image in the *Hieroglyphica.* We can find the woman with the lion on the fourteenth-century Cary-Yale Visconti deck, a hand-painted deck that was made for the rulers of Milan. The other famous Milanese deck, the Visconti-Sforza, has an image of Hercules himself clubbing the lion. A man wrestling with a lion can also be found on some early woodcut decks. On the hand-painted Gringonneur deck and the printed Rosenwald Tarot we find an image for strength that is more common in Renaissance art: a lady holding a large stone column, perhaps breaking it. This is a reference to Samson breaking the pillars of the temple of the Philistines.

Tarot Wisdom

St. Jerome stands busy at work on his translation while his lion sleeps at his feet. The lion represents physical strength. Jerome overpowers the lion not by force but through love. In classical philosophy, strength is the virtue associated with the heart. It is the source of both love and courage; the root of the word *courage* is *cor,* which means "heart." This card represents discipline, courage, and love without fear.

XII ▪ St. Blandina ▪ The Hanged One

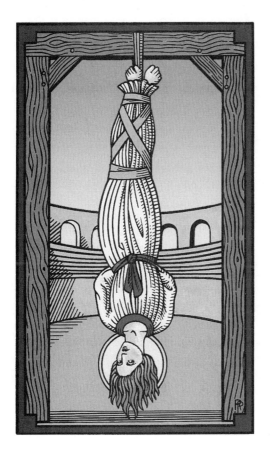

Virtue is like precious odours—most fragrant when they are incensed or crushed.

Francis Bacon

Like the Hanged Man in the Tarot, St. Blandina had to bear condemnation, torture, and public humiliation. Her legend reads like a horror story, but she is one of many heroes who had to face suffering and death for the sake of their spiritual journey.

Who Was Hung in the Arena

Because of slanderous rumors, the people of Lyons in the second century were fearful of Christians. If Christians dared to show themselves in public, they ran the risk of exciting animosity. Blandina was a slave and a Christian serving a Christian master. When her master and several others were arrested for declaring their faith, Blandina was arrested with them. During the trial they were accused of many atrocious crimes including cannibalism and were sentenced to torture and death. Because Blandina was frail, her companions doubted that she would remain steadfast under torture. However, she endured more suffering than the others and remained faithful to the end. She was beaten until her tormentors were exhausted, hung by her feet in the arena to be eaten by wild animals (who refused their meal), and tied in a net and thrown to wild steer. Finally, she was killed with a dagger.

St. Blandina is the patron of torture victims and those who are falsely accused. Her feast day is July 11.

The Tarot Card

The figure of a man hanging by one foot (or sometimes both feet) that appears in all the early Tarot cards is often confusing to modern commentators. Court de Gebelin thought that it had been turned upside down by uninformed card makers and might have originally represented the missing virtue, prudence, standing on one foot to avoid a snake. Once again, the historic evidence does not support his theory. In Renaissance Italy, this figure would have been easily recognized as a traitor—the Minchiate even labels the card "The Traitor." In Italy, the punishment for a traitor was to be hung by the feet (or foot), possibly after execution (this is what happened to Mussolini in World War II after he was executed). It was also the practice to label a person a traitor by having a picture printed of them hanging by the foot and posting it in public. These were called *shame pictures*. Pope John XXIII had one made of Francesco Sforza, the ruler of Milan.

In ancient Rome the government and the state religion were one, and to worship the gods of the state was a patriotic obligation. This was not a problem for members of polytheistic religions who could always add another god to their devotions. However, Christians, whose religion denied the existence of the Roman gods, were considered atheists, and if they refused to worship the gods of the state, they could be accused of treason. As a Christian, St. Blandina was considered a traitor to the state religion of Rome and therefore received a traitor's punishment, being hung by her feet in the arena.

Tarot Wisdom

St. Blandina hangs by her feet in the arena awaiting her fate. Although St. Blandina bears her ordeal calmly for she knows she will triumph in the afterlife, it is still an ordeal. This card can represent suffering or simply an uncomfortable situation. Often the situation is for our own good or betterment in the end.

XIII ▪ St. Stephen ▪ Martyrdom

Men fear death as children fear to go in the dark; and as that natural
fear in children is increased with tales, so is the other.

Francis Bacon

Christ set an example when he sacrificed his life for humanity. In
imitation of him, almost all the earliest saints were martyrs. To love
Christ more than life and to die for one's faith were the qualities that
the first Christians looked for in a hero, and their first hero was St.
Stephen.

The First Christian Martyr

St. Stephen was a Greek-speaking Jew who converted to Christianity. His name in Greek is *Stephanos* which means "crown," and he was the first disciple of Jesus to receive the martyr's crown.

St. Stephen was one of the first seven deacons ordained by the apostles. Deacons administered to the needs of the community and aided the poor. While completing his duties, he worked many miracles in the name of God and spoke with such wisdom and grace that he made many converts to the new religion. Because of his Hellenistic background and his refusal to see God as limited to one place or culture, he was instrumental in spreading Christianity to the Hellenistic community. His views also earned him the wrath of the Jewish Council of Elders who put him on trial for blasphemy. During his trial, Stephen so enraged the council with his statements criticizing the Temple of Jerusalem that they dragged him out of the city and stoned him to death. As he died, Stephen fell to his knees and begged God not to punish his enemies for killing him.

St. Stephen is the patron of deacons, headache sufferers, masons, and horses. His feast day is the day after Christmas, December 26.

The Tarot Card

This card is traditionally titled *La Morte* in Italian, *La Mort* in French, and *Death* in English. In most early decks, including decks that have titles on the other trumps, this card is left untitled for fear of repeating the name of the subject. The Death card has consistently carried a skeletal figure known as the Grim Reaper. In the earliest cards he is standing or riding on a pale horse, a possible reference to death as one of the Four Horsemen of the Apocalypse found in Revelation. The Grim Reaper's weapon of choice is the scythe, but in the Visconti-Sforza deck he uses a bow and arrow. This image of death developed in the mid-thirteenth century in France and was made popular by the Dance of Death, an allegorical dance or work of art in which death is seen to triumph over individuals of every age and class. In the fourteenth-century hand-painted Goldschmidt cards we can find death symbolized by the now familiar skull and crossed bones, the same symbol that we see under the feet of St. Stephen here. In the Tarot the Death card is always in the middle of the sequence, usually numbered thirteen; it is never at the end. Unlike the *Danse Macabre,* the Tarot, as explained in chapter 3, is a triumph in which death loses to a greater trump.

Tarot Wisdom

St. Stephen stands on a pile of rocks, the instrument of his death, holding a palm, the symbol of victory held by martyred saints. On his Bible is the symbol of Christ's martyrdom, and at his feet the rose—a symbol of perfection and life triumphing over death—grows from the skull. St. Stephen represents the defeat of death. He sees the end as a new beginning, the beginning of the afterlife.

In its simplest meaning, the Martyrdom card representing death symbolizes the end of something. Whenever it emerges in a reading, it is pointing to the end of a situation and to a new beginning. It does not predict physical mortality and it should not be feared.

As St. Stephen also symbolizes martyrdom itself, this may be another meaning of the card. Are you being asked to sacrifice your interests for a greater good or is this an indication that you are too willing to play the martyr and should strive for self-fulfillment? Look to the surrounding cards for the answer.

XIV ▪ St. Benedict ▪ Temperance

To pray is to work, to work is to pray.

Ancient motto of the Benedictine Order

Unlike many of the martyrs and ascetics of the early Church, St. Benedict set an example of harmony and moderation. He was a master of the art of living, who, like Buddha, saw that extreme asceticism was yet another trap of the ego.

The Wellspring of Temperance

St. Benedict was born to a Roman noble family in Umbria in 480. He studied in Rome where he was disappointed in the disorderliness and lack of discipline of his fellow students. In search of a purer life, he fled to the mountains near Subiaco and lived as a hermit. During that time, it is said that he was fed by a raven (his companion on the Tarot card). News of his virtue spread, and when the local abbot died, he was asked to take over his position. However, the monks found his rule too severe and one day tried to kill him by putting poison in his drink. When St. Benedict lifted the glass and made the sign of the cross over it, the glass broke and saved him from death. After this incident, St. Benedict returned to the hermit's life, but the miracle of the broken glass only added to his reputation and he continued to attract followers. Eventually, he established twelve monasteries.

St. Benedict wrote the rule of monastic law that bears his name. His rule was almost the only monastic code to be used by most monasteries in the Middle Ages. It is characterized by the virtues of prudence and temperance. St. Benedict believed that the occupation of the monk was to pray, but to accomplish this, time had to be allotted for all necessities as well. He used the water clock (symbolized by the water-driven hourglass on the card) to regulate all aspects of a monk's life. There was a time to sleep; a time to work at carpentry, in the garden, or on manuscripts; a time to eat; a time to study; and a time to pray. Prayers were sung and scheduled at six intervals during the day.

St. Benedict died of a fever when he was in his sixties. In his life, he helped to create the medieval monastic system and guaranteed that it was a center of health and well-being that preserved art and learning. He is credited with the gift of prophecy, particularly the ability to forestall attacks by the devil (which is in keeping with his place in this deck).

St. Benedict is the patron of agriculture, monks, coppersmiths, and people suffering from poisoning, inflammatory diseases, and nettle rash. His feast day was March 21 but is now July 11.

The Tarot Card

The Tarot card consistently shows the virtue temperance as a woman pouring water from one vessel to another. In the Tarot of Marseilles, she is given wings. This is the common image of temperance that we find depicted in Renaissance art.

To the ancients, temperance was the regulation of desire. It was the primary virtue that Plato felt was necessary for all the workers in his ideal republic to develop. To learn temperance, Plato recommended learning music, and from the ancient world to the Renaissance, temperance has been considered the mother of the arts. In the Renaissance mind, the balancing of desires was closely connected to the physical balance of the four humors. The humors were part of Renaissance medicine and they consisted of four bodily liquids (phlegm, blood, and black and yellow bile) that were related to the four elements. When these liquids were in proper balance one was said to be in "good humor" or able to "hold one's temper." The Tarot Temperance figure is creating balance by proportioning liquid between her two vessels.

From the ancient world to the Renaissance, the primary way of measuring time was by the use of a clock that was driven by water pouring from one vessel into another. Temperance can be interpreted as regulating time in this way with the use of a water clock. She is sometimes called the angel of time, and timing is essential to the art of music.

Temperance can also mean sobriety and her action on the card can be interpreted as adding water to wine to make it less intoxicating. This is exactly what the priest does in mass, which symbolizes the water of baptism mixing with the blood of Christ. Water can be seen as the symbol of life and hope and wine as death and fear. By mixing them we can come to the peace beyond hope and fear, to the temperance that is not the slave of the emotions.

Tarot Wisdom

On the card, St. Benedict stands with his raven at his side pouring water into his clock, regulating life at his monastery and assuring that there will be intervals in the day for song. Temperance means balance and beauty. It is the regulation of time and the ability to be on time. It represents finding peace and not being driven by our emotions.

XV ▪ St. Margaret and The Devil

Yea, though I walk through the valley of the shadow of death, I will
fear no evil: for thou art with me.

Psalm 23:4

St. Margaret's story is so fantastic it is not surprising that her veneration has been suppressed. However, with her calm joyful attitude in
the face of danger, St. Margaret is an illustration of the 23rd Psalm.
In the *Tarot of the Saints,* it is difficult to assign a saint to the Devil

card, but St. Margaret's dealings with the devil certainly qualify her for this position.

Who Was Swallowed by the Devil

According to legend, St. Margaret was born the daughter of a Pagan priest in Antioch. When she became a Christian she was thrown out of her home and lived as a shepherdess. Olybrius, the governor of Antioch, was taken by her beauty and carried her off to his palace to seduce her. Of course, she refused him and declared that she was married to Christ and to chastity. In his anger, Olybrius had her fed to a dragon. Margaret bore her fate with calm assurance. Once she was swallowed she burst open the belly of the dragon and stepped out triumphant. Some say that she used her crucifix to cut open the belly. She continued preaching and making converts until she was beheaded by Diocletian.

In the Bible, the devil is depicted as a dragon or serpent. The horned figure with the pitchfork that we usually find in the Tarot is a product of art. In medieval and Renaissance art, we also often find images of a dragon's head with a gaping mouth swallowing people. These images, called *Hell Mouths,* represent the gate of Hell swallowing the condemned. In this light, Margaret's ordeal is a trip to Hell and back. This trip to the dark recesses and a confrontation with evil is part of the symbolism of the alchemical great work as well. It is symbolism that echoes images from the ancient world in which an individual being swallowed by a serpent was a symbol of the process of initiation into the mysteries. To go through this process and attain gnosis was to be reborn, and that is exactly what Margaret does when she bursts out of the belly. Perhaps that is why she is associated with childbirth.

St. Margaret is the patron of women, pregnant women, women in labor, nursing mothers, peasants, martyrs, and those who need to escape from the devil. Before her veneration was suppressed, her feast day was July 20 in the West and July 13 in the East.

The Tarot Card

The Devil is absent in the early hand-painted decks. However, we have examples of him in early Italian printed cards. In the Bible, Satan is depicted as a serpent or a dragon, but he never appears in that form in the early Tarot. Instead, the Tarot artists drew from the rich body of demonic imagery present in Gothic art. On the cards, the Devil appears as a horned humanoid figure sometimes with bird feet and a face in place of his genitals. He may be brandishing a pitchfork or devouring his victims. In the French decks based on the Tarot of Marseilles, the figure becomes somewhat standardized. He is a figure with horns or antlers and bat wings and most often holds a torch. He seems to have the breasts of a woman and the genitals of a man and sometimes a face on his abdomen. Two smaller minions, possibly one male and one female, are chained to his pedestal.

To the Gnostics, the devil was the creator and ruler of the physical world. His job is to keep us from achieving the freedom of enlightenment. This is similar to the role of Mara in the story of Buddha's enlightenment. The Devil appearing here, at the beginning of the third section of the trumps, is the gateway to higher realms. We have to deal with the devil if we want to progress. As Dante demonstrated in the *Divine Comedy*, the way to Heaven is through Hell.

Tarot Wisdom

St. Margaret stands in front of the devil, his mouth surrounding her like the gate of Hell, but Margaret is poised, calm, and serene. She does not fear evil because her faith is strong. The Devil represents a bad situation, something that enslaves or traps us like a dead-end job or an addiction. It can be a relationship that we do not want to be in or something that is harmful or self-destructive. During World War II, the statesman Winston Churchill once expressed the idea that if one is in Hell, it is best to continue the journey until that is no longer the case. St. Margaret agrees and assures us that we have the power to break free to come through stronger for the experience.

XVI ▪ St. Barbara ▪ The Tower

Our friends, then, are all those who unjustly afflict us with trials and ordeals, shame and injustice, sorrows and torments, martyrdom and death; we must love them greatly for we all possess eternal life because of them.

St. Francis of Assisi

St. Barbara's veneration began in the seventh century. Although St. Barbara was one of the most popular saints of the Middle Ages, it is doubtful that her story is based on a historical person. For this reason, she was removed from the Church calendar in 1968. Her story has many details in common with the drawing on the Tower card, and it is possible that her story was a source of inspiration for the image.

Held in a Tower

According to her legend, Barbara was the daughter of a rich Pagan named Dioscorus so she kept her Christianity secret. Her father, recognizing her great beauty, decided to lock her in a tower for her own good and kept it carefully guarded. Word of the mysterious beauty locked in a tower got out and an intrigued suitor made a formal offer of marriage through her father. Dioscorus, considering the suitor a suitable prospect, reported the offer to his daughter. Barbara, however, refused the offer because she had taken an oath of chastity as a proclamation of her faith. Her father, annoyed by her refusal, became suspicious that his daughter was hiding something from him.

After some time, Dioscorus left on a business trip, but before going he commanded that a bath be built for her use in the tower. During his absence, Barbara charmed the workers with her grace and convinced them to install three windows in the tower as a symbol of the Holy Trinity. When her father returned he immediately saw the three windows and questioned his daughter about its significance. She acknowledged herself to be a Christian. Dioscorus was outraged and dragged her before the prefect of the province, Martinianus, who had her cruelly tortured and finally condemned her to death by beheading. Barbara's father carried out the death sentence himself. He brought Barbara to the top of the tower and cut off his daughter's head with a sword. As he completed his gruesome task, a bolt of lightning struck him dead. After Barbara was buried, numerous healings and miracles were attributed to her and she was declared a saint.

St. Barbara is the patron of architects, gunners, artillerymen, firefighters, fireworks makers, and miners, and is called on for protection from lightning and sudden death. Martyrologies in the ninth century, with exception of one by Rabanus Maurus, place her feast day on December 16. On modern calendars until the time of the suppression of her veneration, St. Barbara's feast day was December 4.

The Tarot Card

The Tower is missing from all the early hand-painted decks except the Gringonneur deck which depicts a tower being struck by fire from above. In some of the printed cards two figures falling from the tower were added, and this became the standard image in the Tarot of Marseilles.

In the Italian decks, it was usually called "Fire" or else "The House of the Devil" or other variations. In Mitelli's *Tarocco Bolognese* and the Belgian Tarot, it was sometimes called "Lightning" or "Thunderbolt" and a fiery lightning bolt would be shown striking a person or tree instead of the tower. In the Tarot of Marseilles, the name of the card is mysteriously changed to *Maison Dieu,* "The House of God."

The central image of the card is a lightning bolt striking down from the sky as divine punishment or destruction. The Tower is sometimes associated with the Tower of Babel, a symbol of pride that God destroyed. We can see that St. Barbara, who is strongly associated with lightning and towers, would naturally be associated with this card as well. Her tower starts as her prison (the House of the Devil), but through her addition of three windows—a detail found on the card in the Tarot of Marseilles—she transforms it to the House of God and her father receives divine punishment in the form of lightning.

Tarot Wisdom

Just as in her icon, St. Barbara on the Tarot card holds her symbol the tower which she has transformed from a prison to the House of God by the construction of three windows. Lightning connects the tower with Heaven, and her father falls from the summit. This card, which comes after the Devil, represents breaking away from the devil's trap. It is transformation, the shattering of illusion, and sudden change. This kind of transformation is abrupt and may be discomforting or unsettling. It may mark the loss of a position, or refer to punishment being awarded for a crime.

XVII ▪ St. Therese ▪ The Star

There is no such thing as bad weather. All weather is good because it is God's.

St. Teresa of Avila

St. Therese's saintliness was subtle and taken for granted during her life, but after her death she delivered the stars.

Who Delivered the Stars

Therese is one of the most popular saints of modern times. She was fifteen when she joined the Carmelite order in Lisieux, the same order that her three sisters joined. Convinced that she was a saint from her earliest childhood, joining the order was her life's ambition.

Her older sisters were part of the Carmelite hierarchy, and for the sake of harmony in the order she was asked to extend her time as a novice. This she did without complaint, and she cheerfully performed the menial tasks that were given to her, such as washing, ironing, and cleaning. Therese went through times of depression and illness but kept this suffering to herself for fear that she would be a burden to others. Her main concern was the perfection of selfless love. Once when accused of a crime she did not commit, she took the blame rather than pass the accusation on to another. To all others, her life seemed unremarkable. The details of her passion were only evident in her journal, but this was not read by anyone until her death.

Therese promised that after she was gone she would unleash a shower of roses in the form of favors and beauty for the world. In her early twenties, she developed tuberculosis, but again kept the symptoms to herself. The illness progressed and became evident to everyone only when it was too late. At the moment of her death at age twenty-three, a fellow sister ran outside to find the night sky dark and overcast. Distraught, the sister asked for a sign from the heavens to commemorate Therese's passing. Instantly the clouds parted to reveal a beautiful array of stars like a stairway to Heaven. During her life, Therese often had expressed her desire to find a stairway to Heaven and it seems that after her death she succeeded. This was the first of numerous miracles that Therese granted. Her diary was edited by her sister, Agnes, and published as *The Story of a Soul*. Because of the everyday simplicity of her striving to express love, Therese's writing has been an inspiration to many people.

St. Therese is the patron of flowers and France. Her feast day is October 3.

The Tarot Card

Once again, Tarot artists at different times have made different associations with this image. The hand-painted Milanese cards contain a goddess-like woman in a long star-speckled dress holding a star over-head. In the uncut sheet in the Metropolitan Museum, a nude male holds the star. In some decks, like the Minchiate, the image is related to the Magi following the star of Bethlehem, and on others we find astronomers.

However, the Tarot of Marseilles contains the most evolved mystical image for this card. The image is of a nude female pouring water from two pitchers, one onto the land and one into the sea. Above her are seven stars situated around a larger eighth one. In the Renaissance, nudity was a symbol of purity and truth. The nude on the Star card can be related to Sophia, the divine wisdom that enables the mystic to make the ascent up the ladder of planets, and the seven stars overhead can represent those planets. The eighth star represents the eighth sphere on which the fixed stars revolve and is considered the gateway to Heaven. Sophia pours water onto the land and into the sea. This is an alchemical symbol representing mastery of the alchemical work through the combination of opposites, a mastery that allowed the spirit to ascend to a higher state. It is based on lines found in Revelation such as, "And the angel which I saw stand upon the sea and the earth lifted up his hand to Heaven" (10:5). In alchemy, this idea can also be represented by the image of the Siren of the Philosophers discussed in the section on St. Catherine. Sophia shows us the place between wet and dry, between our hopes and fears. Behind her, a bird, the symbol of the soul, sits in a tree.

Tarot Wisdom

St. Therese stands with her hands across her breast in acceptance of God's grace. Above her the clouds part and the ladder of the planets shows us the way to Heaven. This is an opportunity to ascend to a higher state. At the mundane level, it represents a breakthrough, an opportunity suddenly becoming available, a calm after a storm, or forgiveness after an argument.

XVIII ▪ ST. MARY ▪ THE MOON

All gifts, virtues, and graces of the Holy Ghost are administered by the hands of Mary to whomsoever she desires, when she desires, in the manner she desires, and to whatever degree she desires. Mary is the dispensatrix of all the graces God bestows. Every grace granted to man in this life has three successive steps: from God it comes to Christ, and from Christ to the Virgin, and from the Virgin it descends to us.

St. Bernadine of Sienna

St. Bernadine's statement depicts Mary as more than the mother of Jesus; she is a living presence in the world, an emanation from God.

Who Stands on the Moon

Mary is called *Theotokos* ("the Mother of God"), the Queen of All Saints, *Madonna* ("Our Lady"), and numerous other titles that were once the epithets of ancient goddesses. Of all the saints, she is the most venerated and receives the most prayers.

Mary is the mother of Jesus and the wife of St. Joseph. According to Church doctrine, Mary was conceived without original sin, called the *Immaculate Conception.* The angel Gabriel came to her to announce the birth of Jesus. She conceived Jesus through the Holy Spirit and gave birth to Jesus as a virgin; thus she is also referred to as the "Blessed Virgin." Mary fled to Egypt with Jesus and Joseph, may have traveled with Jesus after their return to Nazareth, and was present at the Crucifixion. At the end of her earthly existence she was taken into Heaven body and soul, which is called the *Assumption.*

For the first five centuries after Christ, Mary's veneration was discouraged by the Church for fear that she would overshadow Jesus. The council of Ephesus in 431 ruled that she could be called "the Mother of God." From the sixth to ninth centuries she achieved her full status and was named "Queen of Heaven." Mary came to be viewed as the matrix of God's grace and forgiveness. By praying to her, sinners could enlist her influence to turn away God's anger.

In one legend, a man named Theophilus sells his soul to the devil in exchange for wealth, but on his deathbed he implores Mary to get the contract back. She does and Theophilus is saved from eternal damnation. The legend was translated into Latin in the eighth century and helped to spread Mary's devotion to the West. Because of her motherly love she was viewed as approachable, and because of Christ's love for his mother he would listen to her. She filled the role in Christianity that mother goddesses did in ancient religions, and in the Western Church, she became the embodiment of Sophia.

Since her first appearance in 1061 in Norfolk, England, Mary began making a series of public apparitions. In most, she takes the form of a woman in white with light radiating from her and instructs the devoted to build a chapel. Later, the chapels become sites of devotion and miraculous healing. The most famous three are the apparition at Guadalupe in 1531, Lourdes in 1858, and Fatima in 1917. In the last 150 years, the number of apparitions has been growing. There have been over two hundred reported in the United States alone in the last one hundred years.

St. Mary is the patron of over sixty countries and each of the fifty states in the U.S., and the patron of the human race, mothers, virgins, air crews, aviators, clothworkers, coffeehouses, construction workers, cooks, goldsmiths, and numerous other occupations. She has numerous feast days, most of which have been reduced in rank since the 1969 Roman calendar. Her principal feast day is January 1, which is devoted to her role in the Incarnation.

The Tarot Card

The Moon card in the Tarot has consistently depicted the feminine celestial body in all decks through the centuries. It is in the associations with the moon that appear on the lower half of the card that they differ. The old Italian Tarot designs include numerous astronomers making measurements or holding a clock, a reference to the moon as the gauge of time. In some decks, we find references to the moon goddess, a woman in a long dress holding the moon, or Diana with her hound. In some naive woodcut decks we find a *putto* (cherub) holding the moon or simply the moon with a face. On an uncut sheet of sixteenth-century Italian printed cards in the library at Yale University we can see one of the oldest examples of the design that was made popular by the Tarot of Marseilles. It depicts a crayfish climbing out of a pool and reaching for the moon. In the French versions, two dogs are added. The crayfish relates to the constellation Cancer, the native house of the moon, and the dogs are Diana's companions in mythology.

Tarot Wisdom

Mary stands on the moon as Queen of Heaven, an image based on her description in Revelation 12:1: "And there appeared a great wonder in Heaven; a woman clothed with the sun, and the moon under her feet, and upon her head a crown of twelve stars." From her hands, she radiates God's grace, love, and forgiveness. She represents unconditional love, forgiveness, night, a time of rest, and mothering. This is not a time to go forward, it is a time to rest and recuperate to be forgiving of ourselves as well as others.

XIX ▪ Christ ▪ The Sun

I am the light of the world; he who follows me will not walk in darkness, but will have the light of life.

John 8:12

Quoted above are the words of Jesus from the Gospel of St. John. The Gospel of St. John begins with another famous line: "In the beginning was the Word." John then goes on to make it clear that the Word is an ordering principle that was present at the creation of the world and that manifested once again in Christ. Although most readers find the opening lines of John poetic and mysterious, they also may find them confusing. What in English is translated as "the Word" in the original Greek is the term *Logos,* and although this English translation is not entirely incorrect, it does not capture the broadness of meaning contained in the original. The meaning of this passage would become clearer if the term *Logos* was presented untranslated and the modern reader became familiar with the totality of its meaning.

Logos was one of the most important concepts in the classical world, often expressed by philosophers and mystics. Its meaning includes the ideas of order, proportion, intelligence, creativity, and harmony. The Logos represents the loving harmony and intelligence of the universe—the force that created the world and that sustains its order and logic. It is like light illuminating the darkness. When we connect with it in a mystical state of oneness we experience enlightenment; therefore, it was commonly symbolized by the sun.[3] Jesus' words quoted above make it clear that he is the manifestation of the Logos; he is the sun that brings enlightenment.

Who Is Like the Sun

Christ is the historic person who was given the name of Jesus at his birth in Nazareth. He is recognized by all Christians as the Christ, a word derived from the Greek *christos* ("the anointed one") and equivalent to the Hebrew title *messiah.* It is central to Christian faith to believe that Christ was crucified on the cross, rose from the dead, and is the son of God incarnate. The resurrected Christ continues to be active as the embodied spirit of God—the light or the Logos—in the world and particularly in the Christian community called "the Church."

Christ, as the Logos, is available to all who open themselves to his love and council. It is the community of saints who can most attest to this. One modern example of this is Blessed Faustina Kawalska, a Polish nun who has been elevated to the second level of the canonization process.

When Faustina was twenty she entered the congregation of the Sisters of Our Lady of Mercy, and devoted herself to prayer and directed all of her prayers to Jesus. In the years before World War II, Faustina received predictions and warnings from Christ, but his primary message was that he wanted her to become an instrument for his divine mercy. Beginning in 1931, Faustina beheld a vision of Jesus with two rays streaming from his heart. One, stemming from his right side, was red symbolizing the blood that he shed to atone for our sins, and the other, from the left, was white symbolizing the water of baptism. Christ asked her to have this image of him painted and to include the inscription "I trust in you" on the bottom. He said that all that viewed the icon with trust would receive his forgiveness and mercy and spread this mercy to others. The Sun card in this deck is based on this image known as the "Divine Mercy icon."

In alchemical texts from the Renaissance, we can find an image of a twin-tailed mermaid with streams pouring from her breasts like a fountain. The stream from her right breast is red and said to be blood and the stream from her left is white and said to be milk. This image is called the "Siren of the Philosophers" and the alchemists believed her to be the gateway to higher consciousness.

The Tarot Card

The Sun card always depicts the masculine celestial orb and is the highest trump before Judgement and the World, symbols of the victory over time and death. In some orders Justice is also included after the Sun, showing the connection between Justice and St. Michael, who is the weigher of souls present at the Last Judgment. As with the Moon, it is on the lower half of the card in early decks that we find different associations. As with other celestial cards, we can find a putto holding the sun. On some, there is a reference to Apollo, the sun god. In several early decks the card shows a woman with a distaff, a stick used for winding wool. This image can be traced to the cosmic myth in the last chapter of Plato's *Republic*. In this myth, the souls of the dead returning to the world to be reincarnated view the goddess Necessity sitting in the center of the cosmos with the axis mundi, around which the sun and other planets spin, sitting in her lap like a spindle.

In the fifteenth-century D'Este deck we find an illustration of the story of the philosopher Diogenes who humbly lived in a barrel. When Alexander the Great paid him a visit and asked if he could do him a favor, Diogenes only requested that Alexander move so as not to block the sun.

In the Minchiate, as in some later decks, we find lovers on this card. In the Tarot of Marseilles, there are two youths. Because of their youth and their loincloths, their sex cannot be determined. The youths may represent a male and female joined together in innocence in a new golden age, or twin males, perhaps the brothers Castor and Pollux of the Gemini constellation, or Romulus and Remus, the founders of Rome. Although Castor and Pollux had the same mother, Leda, Castor's father was mortal which made Castor mortal, and Pollux's father (Zeus) was immortal, which made Pollux immortal. In the myth of the founders of Rome we find the same polarity. After the brothers founded Rome, Remus died but his brother never did, and after forty years of rule Romulus vanished and became the god Quirinus. So whether the pair is masculine or feminine or mortal and immortal they represent the joining of opposites, what the alchemists call the *greater conjunction,* a state of unity that precedes the final mystical state. This same unity in the mystical experience of the One is expressed in the Divine Mercy icon.

Tarot Wisdom

Christ stands in the doorway beckoning us to enter. He is our guide to our inner peace and strength. From his heart come the red and white rays of forgiveness, representing our fears and hopes and showing that he is the unity beyond the aimless striving of our lives. This card can represent forgiveness, a chance to improve, a new direction, or insight. Suddenly the lights are on and we can see. Because his twin lights represent the duality that occupies the unenlightened mind most of the time, this can be a card of instruction, with a card representing our fears to the red side and a card representing our hopes to the white side.

XX ▪ St. Gabriel ▪ Judgement

Come ye blessed of my father inherit the kingdom prepared for you from the foundation of the world.

Matthew 25:34

The words of Christ from the Gospel of St. Matthew quoted above are an invitation to Heaven extended to all deserving people, living and dead. This call is meant to accompany the music of Gabriel's trumpet on the day of judgment and has the power to raise the dead from their tombs.

The Angel of Judgment

The archangels Gabriel, Michael, and Raphael are the only angels to be called saints. St. Gabriel's name means "God is my strength." He is the guardian of the celestial treasury, and is known as "the Angel of Redemption" and "the Chief Messenger of God." In his role as messenger, St. Gabriel tended to the infant Abraham, sent word through Daniel of the return of the Jews from captivity, foretold the birth of Samson, announced to Elizabeth the birth of St. John, announced to Mary the birth of Jesus, and dictated the Koran to Muhammad. Through these activities, Gabriel has been instrumental in founding three major world religions (Judaism, Christianity, and Islam), thus demonstrating that they are all branches from the same trunk. It is traditionally believed that his final announcement will be the trumpet call of the Last Judgment.

St. Gabriel is the patron of the telephone, telegraph, and postal workers. His feast day is September 29.

The Tarot Card

In almost all decks this card represents Judgment Day—also known as the Second Coming—when Christ will return, the dead will rise from their graves, and all will be judged and sent to their final reward or punishment. This is a popular image in medieval and Renaissance churches, one of the most famous being Michelangelo's painting on the wall behind the altar of the Sistine Chapel. The cards do not try to capture the complexity of this theme like church murals do. Instead, they focus exclusively on one scene: the raising of the dead. In the hand-painted Italian decks we find two angels with trumpets hovering over open graves with three to seven men and women waking from death. The Visconti-Sforza deck adds God the Father to the scene. In printed decks, the image becomes more uniform. There is one trumpeting angel above and two to four people emerging from their graves below. In the Tarot of Marseilles and its offshoots, the number of the risen is always three.

The Minchiate substitutes the image of Fame on this card. Fame is depicted as an angel flying over a landscape carrying two trumpets, one for fame and one infamy. In Renaissance art, the first trumpet is often golden and the other common wood or bronze. The substitution of Fame as an alternative points out that the theme of this card in both variations is a triumph over death; both of these images represent immortality.

Tarot Wisdom

St. Gabriel flies over a cemetery sounding his trumpet. From the graves, we see three bodies in three different stages of reanimation. This card is a call to a higher state of being. On a worldly level, this card signifies calling up the past, making decisions based on experience, or simply reminiscing. It can also refer to revitalizing parts of ourselves that we have blocked or denied.

XXI ▪ St. Sophia ▪ The World

Happy is the man that findeth Wisdom, and the man that getteth understanding:

For the merchandise of it is better than the merchandise of silver, and the gain thereof than fine gold.

She is more precious than rubies: and all the things thou canst desire are not to be compared to her.

Length of days is in her right hand; and in her left hand riches and honor.

Her ways are pleasantness, and all her paths are peace.

She is a Tree of Life to them that lay hold upon her: and happy is every one that retaineth her.

> *The lord by Wisdom has founded the earth; by understanding hath*
> *he established the heavens.*
>
> Proverbs 3:13–19

Sophia means "wisdom" in Greek. We could substitute her name wherever it says *wisdom* in the above quotation from Proverbs, and this is how it would have appeared to the early Hellenistic Christians. Sophia has lent her name to the word *philosophy*, which is the love of her, and to the Gnostics she represents the soul of the world.

Holy Wisdom

In the Western hagiographies, St. Sophia is the mother of the virgin martyrs Faith, Hope, and Charity. Three days after the death of her daughters, Sophia passed peacefully away while praying by their tombs. This legend is believed to be an allegory. Sophia's role as sacred wisdom is clearly defined in the East; the primary cathedral of Byzantium in Constantinople was named after her. However, it is in Gnostic literature that we can find her greatest significance.

To Aristotle, Sophia was the highest of the virtues. She represented the spiritual aspect of the intellect that manifested itself in contemplation and allowed the divine nature hidden in all humans to emerge. Jewish mystics of the fourth century B.C. feared erosion of their religion as many Jews turned toward Greek philosophical rationalism. In answer to this challenge, these fourth-century writers crafted an image of Sophia (written as *Hokmah* in Hebrew and *Sophia* by the Greek-speaking Jews) as the wisdom of God—a part of God, yet a separate female personality. The wisdom embodied in the Jewish Sophia was a mystical acceptance of God beyond the rational. She also served the function of providing an image of the divine feminine.[4]

Originally the Jewish religion was not truly monotheistic, and it made a place for the divine feminine. For example, in the temple of Solomon was a statue of the Canaanite fertility goddess Asherah, and many of the worshippers of Yahweh considered Asherah Yahweh's wife.[5] By the fourth century B.C., the role of Yahweh had grown until he was considered the one and only God. In this climate, Sophia fulfilled the Jews' yearning for the missing feminine aspect of the divine.

Although the details vary from one account to another, Sophia became prominent in the Gnostic creation myths. She was said to be the first or the thirteenth emanation from the true God and the mother of all the angels, called *aeons*. Through an initial catastrophe, which varies in different texts, she became trapped in the world of matter and longed to return to God. Once in this world, she transmigrated into different female bodies and suffered various indignities—she was assaulted, raped, and trapped in a brothel. Her trials and tribulations ended when she fell into remorse and sought redemption. Her love of the light of lights, the Logos who is embodied in Christ, is restored. Christ returned her to the higher realm where she became his bride in a mystical marriage. It is easy to see how her myth was grafted onto Mary Magdalen; if Jesus is the Logos, then Mary is Sophia.

The myth of the divine feminine being trapped in or permeating matter is an archetype found in pre-Christian religions. Sophia relates to the Shekinah in Judaism, another feminine aspect of God that became prominent in the fourth century B.C. The Shekinah was considered to be the spirit of God in the world. The same archetype can be found in the Zoroastrian Daena, a feminine image of the soul; and the Greek Psyche (soul), who searches through the world to be reunited with her love, Eros. Mystics from all traditions have continued to identify with Sophia and use her name. To see her is synonymous with the experience of gnosis. In the Tarot she is the Anima Mundi depicted on the World card. She represents the soul of the world redeemed by the mystical quest. She is gnosis, she is enlightenment, she is the wisdom that our true being is unconditional, eternal, and absolute.

St. Sophia does not have a patronage. Instead, she represents wisdom and is the mother of Christian virtue. Her feast day is September 30.

The Tarot Card

The World card from the Tarot of Marseilles tradition depicts the Anima Mundi in a quincunx (see chapter 3). In the early hand-painted decks, the Anima Mundi is depicted as a queen hovering above the Earth and is represented by a circle or an arch containing a landscape. On the Visconti-Sforza card and another following the same model, two putti hold the circle of the world overhead. A fifteenth-century printed deck in Paris and the Tarocchini di Bologna both have a figure that is possibly Hermes. Most of the earliest printed decks have angels that are androgynous but lean toward being female. The French Jacques Vievil deck has a male figure that is possibly Christ. The symbolism on these other World cards is not necessarily a quincunx. However, it consistently represents the spirit or soul of matter; most often is it female, less often is it androgynous, and more rarely is it male. Often the figure relates to the world as an axis mundi or sovereign of the sacred center, which, although not being a quincunx, is a related symbol. The World exposes the truth that the world is sacred and therefore we are sacred.

Tarot Wisdom

St. Sophia stands in a mandorla, an almond-shaped aura that represents heavenly radiance. She stands on a globe and in front are the symbols of the three Christian virtues, her daughters Faith, Hope, and Charity symbolized by the cross, the anchor, and the heart. To the four cardinal points are the symbols of the Four Evangelists, which are said to surround the throne of Christ in the Book of Revelation. The symbols can be equated to the four elements, directions, and cardinal virtues using Figure 4.1. The four creatures, symbolizing the four cardinal virtues, combined with the symbols of the three Christian virtues provide all seven rungs on the ladder leading to the vision of the One.

At the highest level, the World represents the experience of the One, the Good, and the Beautiful—an attainment of oneness with

Evangelist	Symbol	Zodiac Sign	Element	Direction	Virtue
Matthew	human	Aquarius	air	west	prudence
Mark	lion	Leo	fire	east	strength
Luke	bull	Taurus	earth	north	temperance
John	eagle	Scorpio	water	south	justice

FIGURE 4.1—Table of correspondences for the Four Evangelists

God. This is called *gnosis* or *enlightenment*. At its simplest level, she represents what is good or desirable, a more enlightened way of behaving or the culmination of our goals. This card represents the good or the sacred.

CHAPTER 5

THE FOURFOLD WORLD

The entire Tarot deck is a quincunx. The four minor suits are related to the material world of the four directions, four seasons, and four elements that surround the sacred center illustrated by the trumps. The four minor suits were a complete game deck that existed before the Tarot was created. The creators of the Tarot simply added the fifth suit to this deck. The suit symbols—coins, swords, cups, and staffs—are still in use in parts of Italy, North Africa, and in Spanish-speaking countries for common playing cards, and they are the ancestors of the French suit symbols, which are also used in English-speaking countries and much of Europe.

Traditionally, the pip cards in the Tarot, which are numbered from ace to ten, carried only depictions of the suit symbol repeated per the card's number like modern playing cards. In the game, the feminine suits—coins and cups—were ranked ace high to ten low, and the masculine suits—swords and staffs—were ranked ace low to ten high. Divinatory meaning could only be determined by the numerological symbolism of the first ten integers combined with associations with each suit symbol. Pictures were first added to the cards by Pamela Colman Smith as an aid for divination for the Waite-Smith deck (also known as the Rider-Waite deck) in 1910. The only historical precedent she had to draw on was the fifteenth-century Sola Busca deck which includes figures interacting with the suit symbols. Smith's deck set a precedence for modern Tarot decks. The *Tarot of the Saints* follows the modern model and has scenes on the bottom of each pip—under the suit symbols—to illustrate the card's divinatory meaning.

The four royal cards in each minor suit of the Tarot rank above the ten pips and they rank as they would have in late medieval society. The lowest is usually translated as the *page* in English. In the Middle Ages and Renaissance, a page referred to the first stage of training to become a *knight*. The son of a noble would become a page at age seven or eight by serving and being taught by a lady of higher rank. At age fifteen or sixteen he would become an apprentice to a knight, and his title would change to *squire*. Since the first royal card serves a knight and is usually illustrated with an older male figure, it should be called a squire. This is the label used in the *Tarot of the Saints*. (Another possible name for this card is *jack* or *knave,* which is a servant of the knight not of noble birth.) The squire serves the knight, and in true chivalrous fashion the knight serves the *queen*. The queen in turn serves the *king*.

In the Middle Ages and Renaissance, the four suits were seen as representing the four classes of society. Connections were commonly made to the four elements, which is demonstrated in the masculine and feminine designations of the suits. In fact, all aspects of the fourfold world can be related to each other. Figure 5.1 gives the associations of each suit with its French suit, social class, element, and per-

Tarot Suit	French Suit	Class	Element	Personality Type
cups	hearts	clergy	water	intuition
swords	spades	nobles	air	thinking
coins	diamonds	merchants	earth	sensation
staffs	clubs	peasants	fire	feeling

FIGURE 5.1—Table of correspondences for the Tarot suits

sonality type. The personality types are based on modern associations from Jungian psychology; see the discussion below.

The fourfold division of society is common to all Indo-European cultures, and is basic to Plato's division of society in his *Republic*. In medieval culture, each class was seen as striving for the virtue embodied by the class above it; peasants strove to attain the temperance of the merchants, the merchants strove to attain the fortitude of the nobles, the nobles strove to attain the judiciousness of the clergy, and the clergy strove to attain the divine virtue prudence.

THE FOUR HUMORS

The ancient Greeks developed a theory of four qualities—hot, cold, dry, and moist—each of which related to two of the four elements. This allowed the Greeks to equate the elements to the seasons, and it also led to associations with four bodily liquids or juices, called *humors*. The four humors were blood, phlegm, black bile, and yellow bile. The humors remained part of medical theory through the Renaissance and their balance was deemed necessary for health and good temperament. Each of the humors was also associated with qualities of personality (Figure 5.2).

The theory of the four humors seems far removed from modern medicine and most people do not realize to what extent this theory has influenced Western culture. However, its influence can be perceived in references to the humors present in modern English words.

Humor	Type	Quality	Element	Temperament
blood	sanguine	hot & moist	air	cheerful
phlegm	phlegmatic	cold & moist	water	sluggish
black bile	melancholic	cold & dry	earth	sad
yellow bile	choleric	hot & dry	fire	vindictive

FIGURE 5.2—Table of correspondences for the four humors

For example, we commonly refer to someone as being "in good humor" or "holding their temper" (a reference to a mix of liquids), words that originally meant that the four humors were in balance. When someone is depressed we say that they are "melancholy," meaning that they have too much black bile, and we might describe a healthy cheerful person as "ruddy" or "rosy-cheeked," meaning that he or she has an abundance of blood, the sanguine humor. In fact, we often look at someone's complexion, a word that originally meant "combination," to determine his or her health and mood. In the Renaissance, the humors were an important part of the people's worldview, and knowledge of them can give us insight into the people who created the Tarot.

PERSONALITY TYPES

The famous psychologist Carl Jung is best known for his pioneering work exploring the unconscious. However, he also succeeded in mapping the conscious mind. Influenced by ancient typology, Jung discovered the internal reality of the fourfold division. He did not consider the classical system a true typology so he created a different system. As shown in Figure 5.1, his four personality types, based on four psychological functions, can be related to the four suits and are a valuable aid to interpreting the cards for divination.

Jung's four psychological functions (or personality types) represent abilities or talents each person has in varying degrees. At birth we are each dealt strengths in one or more of these functions and are therefore weak in the others. Everyone tends to use their strong suit to solve problems and are at a disadvantage when their weak suit is what the situation demands. Each function can be expressed in an introverted (looking within for direction) or extraverted (looking to others for direction) way. Throughout life, if an individual matures, he or she will develop more functions and become more versatile in his or her capabilities. This maturing is what Jung calls the process of *individuation,* a progression toward psychic wholeness that he equates to the hero's journey. If an individual can develop all four functions, then the fifth element of the true self is attained, which is likened to the experience of the Anima Mundi or Christ within. The following is a list of each function with its associated suit and a description.[1]

Intuition—Cups is a talent for determining how a situation developed and where it is headed in the future. It is investigation directed toward the unconscious, which is often symbolized by water, which is associated with the suit of cups in the Tarot. The introvert may tend toward roles of poet, mystic, or psychic. The extravert would be more comfortable investigating society's unconscious and may become an adventurer or entrepreneur.

Thinking—Swords is intellectual. It asks why or what is reality. This is a decision-making function. The introvert may tend toward roles of philosopher or research scientist, and the extravert toward economist, judge, or statesman or stateswoman. Thinking is forceful but intangible like air, the element associated with the suit of swords in the Tarot.

Sensation—Coins simply asks if a thing exists and displays a talent for manipulating it. This is an investigation of the physical world, symbolized by earth, the element associated with the suit of coins in the Tarot. The introvert may tend toward roles of artist, connoisseur, or technician, and the extravert toward engineer, accountant, builder, or investigator.

Feeling—Staffs is often misunderstood. To Jung, feelings are not emotions. He calls emotions "effects" and they can arise from any function. Feelings do not create effects in the face or body. They are a decision-making function that determines if something is good or bad and motivates one to action, symbolized by fire, the element associated with the suit of staffs in the

Tarot. Crying is an emotion, fear is a feeling; laughter is an emotion, joy is a feeling. An introvert may display talents as a healer, nurturer, musician, or monk. An extravert may become a singer, social organizer, or politician.

Notice that intuition and sensation are used to investigate reality. Because of this, they are called irrational. They are equated to the feminine, passive elements of water and earth. The other two functions—thinking and feeling—are decision-making functions. They are called rational, and they are equated to the masculine, active elements of fire and air.

THE QUALITIES OF NUMBERS

The pips in the Tarot are traditionally interpreted through associations with the qualities of each number. These associations can be traced back to the theories of Pythagoras, but they have evolved and changed over the centuries. A list of each number with its association follows.

> **Ace:** Monad, truth, beginnings, start of something new, a seed, essence, life, pattern, potential.

> **Two:** Dyad, formation, polarity, coming together of opposites, equality, inequality, ratio, balance, stagnation, harmony, attraction.

> **Three:** Triad; creation of two-dimensional reality, growth, energy, creativity, and fertilization; three-part structure—having a beginning, middle, and end; the mean between extremes; perfection; the All.

> **Four:** Tetrad, physical manifestation of the three-dimensional, practical attainment, commitment, the key to nature, the four-

fold division of the world—four elements, seasons, and directions.

Five: Pentad, the *quinta essentia,* spirit entering matter, imbalance—upset in equilibrium, change, growth, light, restructuring, justice.

Six: Hexad, harmony, balance, love, male-female union, Aphrodite, Amphitrite, peace, nurturing.

Seven: Heptad, Athena, the hero's journey, battle, development of soul, facing complex choices, evolution, ascension and descension, defense.

Eight: Octad, the recreation of the physical, labor, steadfast, practicality, balance, harmony.

Nine: Ennead, attainment, perfection, prosperity, bringing things to an end, completion, sacrifice, letting go, greatness.

Ten: Decad, the One—eternity, God, the end result of a phase or cycle, resurrection—beginning over again, the All—the many returning to the one or becoming a unit, justice, Nemesis, destiny, immortality.

The Tarot works best when the reader allows him- or herself to interpret the images on the cards spontaneously during each reading instead of merely memorizing the meanings for each card from the book. However, this process is not just free association. It is a synthesis of knowledge of the symbols in the Tarot with personal meaning. To develop a creative understanding of the Tarot symbols it is essential to understand both the symbolism on each card and the symbolic patterns present in the structure of the deck. This chapter has focused on information that will help one gain perspective on the structure of the entire deck. In the next chapter we will discuss each card of the minor suits individually.

CHAPTER 6

THE MINOR SUITS

Following is a discussion of the imagery and divinatory meaning for each card in the minor suits. All cards represent patterns of energy or behavior that are at times called for and at other times not needed or represent excess. Therefore, although some cards may depict images or events that seem unpleasant in comparison to others, there are no truly good or bad cards. Like the trumps, all of the royal cards are represented by a saint. Their individual stories can be inspirational or instructive, and learning them will add richness and depth to a reading.

It is not necessary to use cards reversed or upside down in a reading, and as with the trumps, no meanings for reversals are given. To understand the reasons for this, please refer to the beginning of chapter 7. If you prefer to use reversed cards, then they may be interpreted in the same way except that the direction of the action expressed by the card will change.

ACE OF CUPS

This symbol is called "The Blood of the Lamb." The sacrificial lamb is a symbol of Christ who redeemed us through his sacrifice. The cup is the chalice of wine that is miraculously transformed into Christ's blood during the mass and has the power to wash away our sins. This card represents renewal, forgiveness, and the ability to find the essence of our soul. In the center of our unconscious mind we can find a sacred gift planted there: sacred seeds that are in each of us and that represent our true purpose.

TWO OF CUPS

Two cups come together with one heart. Two individuals become as one. This card represents love, goodness, and prosperity.

THREE OF CUPS

Mary Magdalen with her two companions approach the tomb of Christ. This card represents people who we can count on, a support group, and help leading to discovery and transformation.

FOUR OF CUPS

The Annunciation is Gabriel's announcement of Mary's role in the Incarnation. The Holy Spirit descends. This card represents the soul animating matter. It can represent the recognition of the role of the unconscious in our physical situation; it can also indicate limitations.

FIVE OF CUPS

The fifth element, the Tree of Knowledge, is added and Adam and Eve are expelled from Eden. The fifth element is the spirit, but the spirit can often be disruptive in our lives. It can shatter the comfortable patterns of behavior that we have built and challenge us to work and grow. This card can represent expulsion, being thrown out, getting fired, or the breaking of illusions. On the positive side, it represents knowledge and the presentation of a challenge.

SIX OF CUPS

Christ washes St. Peter's feet. This card represents love, nurturing, and humility.

SEVEN OF CUPS

One vessel stands out from the other. It is a ciborium, the container for the consecrated hosts. On its front is the monogram of Christ. When presented with a choice, one path will stand out. It is the best path because it is one with our inner purpose. We will know it because it feels good.

EIGHT OF CUPS

King David sings the psalms. This card represents creativity, joy, a creative occupation, or a performer.

NINE OF CUPS

A woman climbs a mountain accompanied by a saint. This card represents putting the past behind us, proceeding with confidence, gaining perspective, and accepting help.

TEN OF CUPS

Christ blesses the children. In the Gospel of St. Mark 10:14, Christ said, "Suffer the little children to come unto me, and forbid them not: for of such is the kingdom of God." This card represents tradition, continuation, belonging to a group, and connections.

St. Eligius ▪ Squire of Cups

St. Eligius makes a cup. St. Eligius was a skilled goldsmith who lived in Limoges, France, in the Middle Ages (circa 588–660). He is noted for the miraculous beauty of his work and for creating more from his materials than it would seem possible. According to legend, when King Clotar II gave him enough gold and other materials to create a throne, he amazed the king by making two golden thrones with the allocated materials. After this, he worked under the king's patronage creating chalices, crosses, and plaques and decorating tombs and shrines. Eligius's work was admired throughout the Middle Ages, but it is uncertain if any of it still survives. He was well-known for the Chalice of Chelles, but this disappeared during the French Revolution.

Later in life, St. Eligius followed the call to priesthood and eventually became a bishop. This led him away from his metal craft, but he was equally successful in his work as a preacher. He founded monasteries in Noyen, Paris, Solignac, and he is known as a pioneer apostle in Flanders.

Eligius lived at a time when Christianity was not yet universally practiced in western Europe. He did much to spread Christianity's message and bring new converts to the growing religion. Unfortunately, his methods often took the form of a war of words against the former religions. He was noted for labeling the religious practices of his Pagan competitors as "superstitions." To his credit, he was also instrumental in ending the institution of slavery.

St. Eligius's symbol is the horseshoe. He is the patron of goldsmiths and metalworkers. His feast day is December 1.

This card represents skill, craft, thrift, and the ability to create our own situation or happiness.

St. John ▪ Knight of Cups

St. John finds a serpent in his cup. St. John was the youngest of the Twelve Apostles and the brother of Peter and James. He is said to be the author of the fourth gospel. Although this has been disputed by modern scholars, there is evidence to support the claim and no clear reason to deny it. Unlike other apostles, John lived into his old age when he had the time and introspection to write about the events that he had witnessed. Because his spirit soars upward in his text, especially when he speaks of Christian love (*agape*), he is symbolized by the eagle. Three epistles and Revelation are also attributed to his authorship, but these are stylistically different than the gospel and this attribution is unlikely.

John was one of the first to witness the Resurrection. After this event, following Christ's instruction, he adopted the Blessed Virgin as his mother. He was prominent in the early Church, and eventually settled in Ephesus where he continuously urged his followers to love one another.

The picture on the card illustrates an event from his life. The Emperor Domitian ordered him to drink a cup of poisoned wine. When John picked up the cup, the poison departed in the form of a snake and he drank it unharmed. He lived a long life and died of natural causes.

St. John is the patron of writers, editors, booksellers, and art dealers, and is prayed to for protection from poison. His feast day is December 27.

This card represents a message or a warning from the unconscious. On a mundane level, it can refer to any message.

St. Clare ▪ Queen of Cups

St. Clare stands before her convent holding a pyx, a vessel that holds the host. St. Clare of Assisi was the daughter of a count. At the age of eighteen she heard St. Francis preach and was so moved by his words that she renounced her possessions and became a nun. At first, she joined a Benedictine convent, but eventually Francis was able to find a house for her next to the church of San Domiano in Assisi. Here she founded the Order of Poor Clares that traveled with the Franciscans and administered to the poor.

St. Clare was the female counterpart of St. Francis; they were married in spirit. Like him, she devoted herself to poverty and service. Her order was the most austere of any at that time; the nuns lived in strict poverty and survived only on alms. In spite of this, the Poor Clares attracted members and soon spread to Bohemia, France, and England. Clare thought of poverty as a privilege instead of a burden and, like Francis, was known for her joyousness and love of nature.

According to legend, Clare's convent was twice in danger of being sacked by the army of Emperor Frederick II, which included Saracen mercenaries. On both occasions, Clare took her pyx and stood at the gate singing and praying. The enemies threw down their arms and fled. This is why she is depicted holding the pyx in her icon.

Because she is known to have made embroidered altar cloths, St. Clare is the patron of embroiderers. She is also the patron of eye health, gilders, goldsmiths, and television. Her feast day is August 11.

This card represents the ability to act on trust, to see something through without having to know the outcome ahead of time. At its deepest level, it represents mystery.

St. Andrew ▪ King of Cups

St. Andrew the Apostle stands on the shore of Lake Genesareth by the Sea of Galilee where he was a fisherman with his brother St. Peter. He holds the symbol of his martyrdom—the X-shaped cross—which is known as the *saltire cross,* or *St. Andrew's cross.* Above his head, the cup of St. John baptizes him.

St. Andrew was a devoted follower of St. John the Baptist, and through him he was introduced to Jesus. Andrew became the first apostle and introduced his brother, St. Peter, to Jesus. Andrew witnessed many of Christ's miracles. Andrew was the first to notice the meager provisions of five loaves of bread and two fishes that were insufficient to feed the five thousand people who had gathered for Passover. When Andrew brought this problem to Christ's attention, Christ miraculously multiplied the loaves and fishes to feed the multitude. Later, Andrew also became a miracle worker. On numerous occasions, he survived the attacks of beasts unscathed and he was said to have the power to strike people blind. He is credited with freeing the inhabitants of Nicea of seven demons, which may be interpreted as an allegory of enlightenment (see the discussion of St. Mary Magdalen in chapter 4).

It is not certain where St. Andrew preached, but a traditional belief states that he brought the word of Christ to Asia Minor, Greece, and north to Poland and Russia. In Scotland, he is believed to have founded a church in the seaside town of Fife which houses his relics. Before the eighth-century Battle of Markle between England and Scotland erupted, his cross appeared in the sky and assured the Scottish victory. Because of that vision, he became the patron of Scotland, and his white *X* against a field of blue appears on the British flag to represent the Scottish people.

St. Andrew was martyred on the saltire cross after he first healed, then converted, the wife of a prominent Pagan who did not appreciate his wife's vow of chastity. He was imprisoned, beaten with seven scourges, and bound to the saltire cross from which he preached for two days before he died.

St. Andrew is the patron of Russia, Scotland, Greece, fishermen, singers, maidens, and unmarried women. His feast day is November 30.

This card represents intuitive faith, perseverance, and the ability to find fulfillment within ourselves.

ACE OF SWORDS

A sword held with the hilt up so that it becomes a cross transforms it from a weapon to a symbol of love, sacrifice, and spirit. Love is the opposite of anger and negativity. To find love and joy, we must control our thoughts, represented by the sword. Our thoughts are normally used as a weapon, attacking the world to determine what is useful or threatening. Once we have let go of anxiety, anger, and lust, the mind becomes still and the weapon becomes a vehicle of ascent.

Two of Swords

Two swords cross. The Holy Spirit presides. When two minds come together to engage in dialogue or debate in peace, then the truth can emerge and wisdom can be found. This card represents a discussion.

THREE OF SWORDS

Three swords pierce the Immaculate Heart of Mary. Swords through the heart represent pain and suffering. From its wound the heart bleeds, and roses form a wreath. Through suffering, one learns to empathize with the suffering of others. In this light, suffering is love, symbolized by the roses.

FOUR OF SWORDS

Four swords are in the air; a hermit sits in meditation. Four, the number of physical manifestation, combined with swords—air and thought—symbolizes meditation. The swords hang in the air like thoughts and feelings, rational functions that are under our control. The hermit lets them alone and his mind calms itself like still water. When we leave our thoughts and feelings alone, we come to the place of calm beyond hope and fear. This card may also represent rest and a retreat.

FIVE OF SWORDS

Jesus raises Jairus's daughter from her deathbed. This card represents healing and the ability to fix what is broken. What we thought was beyond repair is resurrected. The spirit is beyond thought or logic.

Six of Swords

Six swords are in the air; a mother protects her daughter from danger and moves with the direction of the blades. This represents protection coming from a higher source and going with the flow.

SEVEN OF SWORDS

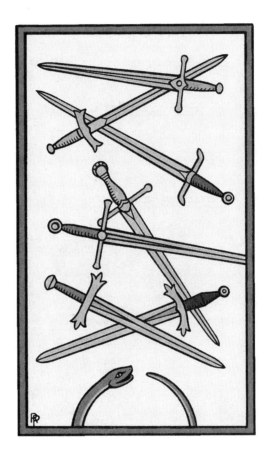

Seven swords are falling and a serpent cannot reach its tail. The seven swords have no pattern. Since it is not biting its tail, the serpent almost, but not quite, forms an ouroboros. This is a time when one order has ended and a new one has not yet formed. It is a time ripe with possibilities and dangers.

EIGHT OF SWORDS

A saint sits in prison; the threat of execution hangs in the air. This card represents imprisonment or blockage. It may also refer to blocked psychic energy.

NINE OF SWORDS

A sword threatens a woman's life. She prays and tries to ignore it. This card represents fear and dread of the future. To instill courage, the mind must be calmed.

TEN OF SWORDS

Ten swords are in the air. Two putti in the foreground hold a banner with the symbol of the five wounds of Christ. The five wounds form a sacred quincunx. Christ's wounds are a badge of honor. This card represents martyrdom, or more commonly, severe criticism. The worst has happened; to move on we must accept our pain. Time is needed to heal.

St. Martin ▪ Squire of Swords

St. Martin of Tours stands holding his sword high after cutting his cloak in half. St. Martin was born in what is now Hungary in approximately 316. His father was a Roman soldier, and like his father, Martin joined the Roman army when he was fifteen. He was stationed in France and once served under Constantine. Eventually, Martin became interested in Christianity and began studying this new faith. One winter Martin came across a naked beggar shivering in the street. He used his sword to cut his cloak and gave half to the beggar. That night in a dream Christ came to him dressed in the half-cloak.

Because of this experience, Martin had himself baptized by Hilary of Poitiers.

St. Martin was convinced that his commitment to Christ was inconsistent with the duties of a soldier, and he attempted to leave the military—one of the first examples of "conscientious objection." For this, his superiors had him imprisoned and his former comrades accused him of cowardliness. In answer to their charges, Martin offered to lead the army into battle armed only with a cross. This declaration of courage won him his freedom and Martin devoted himself to the life of a hermit.

In 372, Martin was appointed Bishop of Tours, although at first he tried to avoid the honor. One Sunday during mass, Martin noticed a poor beggar standing in the midst of his congregation. Martin approached the man and gave him his robe to wear. Then returning to the altar, he raised up the chalice to continue the mass. As he did so, the congregation was stunned to see a golden light envelop his body.

St. Martin is the patron of tailors, drunkards, innkeepers, beggars, equestrians, and France. His feast day is November 11.

St. Martin's story illustrates the following quotation from the Gospel of St. Matthew 25:40: "Truly I say to you, as you did to the least of my brethren, you did it to me." This card represents beauty of action and sincerity of thought.

St. George ▪ Knight of Swords

St. George stands in armor in front of the body of the dragon he has slain. St. George is the model of chivalry. His story, called the "Golden Legend," starts with a poisonous dragon that was terrorizing the countryside in the province of Lybia. The people of the area would feed the dragon two sheep a day to keep it satiated, but when they ran out of sheep they grew fearful that the dragon would devastate the country. Blinded by their fear, they agreed to appease the dragon by feeding it a maiden and held a lottery to determine the victim. It turned out that the princess of the kingdom was the unlucky winner, and her father the king, seeing no way out of his pledge of support, gave permission for his daughter to be led to the dragon's den to await her fate.

At this time, St. George had been traveling looking for ways to use his great strength and ability to right wrongs and defend the weak. He happened on the kingdom during the lottery and observed what was happening. Seeing a chance to live up to his pledge, he hid himself near the gruesome den and watched as the princess was tied to the stake normally used for sheep. As the dragon appeared, George charged in on his stallion, pierced the dragon with his lance, and slayed it with his sword. Everyone was overjoyed and the king gave George a large reward. George could have easily asked for the princess's hand in marriage as well and received half of the kingdom as a dowry, but instead he humbly gave the money to the poor and rode away.

St. George is the patron of knights, chivalry, archers, armorers, horsemen, butchers, plague victims, England, Germany, Portugal, Canada, and the Boy Scouts. His feast day is April 23.

St. George is a hero saint like the heroes of the ancient world. He identifies what is evil and destroys it. For him life is black and white. Sometimes a hero is what is called for, but this is not a good way to approach minor problems. Is what you are trying to destroy truly evil, like the dragon, or is this only an illusion?

St. Joan • Queen of Swords

St. Joan of Arc stands in armor, her sword at her side and holding her cross to her breast. St. Joan is called the "Maid of Orleans." She lived during the Hundred Years' War in Champagne, France. From the age of thirteen, she had visions of St. Michael, St. Catherine, and St. Margaret. In 1428, her divine patrons told her she was destined to save France from the English and restore the true king, the dauphin, to the throne. With the sincerity of her belief, and divine guidance which allowed her to recognize the dauphin while in disguise, she convinced the prince to let her lead the army.

Dressed in white armor, St. Joan inspired the troops to victory in Orleans, captured the English forts in the surrounding area, and went on with her troops to win at Patay. She succeeded in restoring the dauphin, now Charles VII, to the throne. However, after the completion of her mission, her success began to wane. She led a failed attack on Paris, and eventually she was captured by the Burgundians. The Burgundians offered to return her for a ransom, but Charles VII made no attempt to save her. Instead, St. Joan was sold to the English who, with the help of the Church, declared her a heretic and burned her while she was tied to a stake. The Church later called this a political crime that should not have received its endorsement. In 1920, St. Joan was canonized.

St. Joan is the patron of captives, rape victims, women soldiers, and France. Her feast day is May 30.

This card signifies optimism, conviction in one's beliefs, and the ability to advance and set things right.

St. Paul ▪ King of Swords

St. Paul stands with a Bible, the symbol of his mission, and a sword, the symbol of his martyrdom. St. Paul was a tent maker and Talmudic student originally named Saul. Saul hated Christians and persecuted them whenever he could, hunting them down, imprisoning them, and sending them to execution. He was said to be one of the accusers at the stoning of St. Stephen, the first martyr. Ironically, on his way to Damascus to root out more Christians he was blinded by a luminous vision of Jesus that knocked him off his horse. Three days later, he regained his sight and had himself baptized with the name Paul.

Paul became as vigorous in his defense of Christianity as he had been in attacking it. He made numerous converts and with St. Peter founded the Church of Rome. It was in Rome that he was martyred by being beheaded with a sword. It is said that milk flowed from his neck at his execution. His severed head bounced three times, and on each bounce a fountain of water emerged from the sacred ground. Today the three fountains are still visible at a site called "Tre Fontana."

St. Paul is the patron of tent makers, evangelists, rope makers, saddle makers, and public relations. His feast day is January 25.

As fourteen of the epistles contained in the New Testament are attributed to him, St. Paul proves that the pen is mightier than the sword; words are more influential than force. He also symbolizes our ability to improve, to become our better self, and find our destiny.

ACE OF COINS

A golden monstrance holds a host that displays the monogram of Jesus—the first three letters of "Ihsus," his name in Greek. This piece of unleavened bread is miraculously transformed during the Eucharist into the body of Christ. It becomes saturated with spirit and is consumed by the celebrants so that they will be united with Christ. It symbolizes the reality that the entire physical world emanates from the unseen world of the soul. This card represents a birth or a new beginning; a cleansing of the spirit.

TWO OF COINS

A host with the name of Christ and a gold coin with the image of Caesar are tied together in a priest's stole. Jesus commanded us to give Caesar his due and God his due, implying that our worldly duties and our spiritual duties are separate. However, we cannot separate our physical needs from our spiritual needs in the same way. We must be practical in our spiritual quest and take care of our health and well-being. This card can also refer to limitations and a situation that is not flowing.

THREE OF COINS

St. Luke, the patron of artists, paints a portrait of the Madonna, the first icon. Above are symbols of material and spiritual support. This card represents patronage and support for artistic or creative work.

FOUR OF COINS

Judas betrays Jesus with a kiss and receives thirty pieces of silver as his reward. The four of the earth suit is too heavily grounded. There are only coins in the sky, no hosts. This card represents selfishness, greed, and betrayal.

FIVE OF COINS

A crippled beggar sits by the side of the road. In the sky, four coins surround the host. This card represents illness and poverty. When the body is deprived, cravings grow stronger and it is harder to find the healing spirit. Christ healed the sick and the lame with the spirit. Without it, we are all sick and lame. Sickness is a message from the soul. Search the soul to find the cure.

SIX OF COINS

In mythology, the pelican was said to feed its young with its own blood. This became a symbol of Christ, who nurtured humanity with his blood. Above, the symbols of the spiritual and the physical are equally placed and interconnected. This card represents generosity, nurturing, and unconditional love. It is how the world is made beautiful.

SEVEN OF COINS

A farmer scatters seeds into the plowed earth. The sun rises to warm the seeds and help them grow. God is like the sun. God's grace will nurture whatever seeds we plant in our lives. To harvest beauty and well-being, we must sow love through acts of kindness.

EIGHT OF COINS

The young Christ works at carpentry with his earthly father St. Joseph. This card represents labor. To be satisfying, labor must bring spiritual rewards as well as monetary.

Nine of Coins

Loaves and fish are presented on a table. At a Passover gathering described in the Gospel of St. John, Jesus fed five thousand people with just five barley loaves and two small fish. This card represents multiplication and abundance. Prosperity and health are available as needed.

TEN OF COINS

This card presents ten coins and no hosts. It is prosperity but it goes beyond the completion symbolized by nine and may become greed. The spirit is missing; there is only the physical. This refers to materialism in all aspects—financial, medical, scientific, and philosophical.

St. Norbert ▪ Squire of Coins

St. Norbert stands on the road, leaving money behind him. St. Norbert was a noble born in 1080. He traveled the world in luxury until one day he narrowly missed being struck by lightning during a storm. In gratitude for his life, Norbert dedicated the remainder of it to God. Norbert gave his money to the poor. Then he sold his estate so that he could give more. Still not satisfied with his piety, Norbert went on a pilgrimage to Rome where he presented himself to Pope Gelasius II, confessed his sins, and asked for penance. The pope was impressed with Norbert, and he authorized him to wander the countryside preaching the gospel. Norbert was well suited to the task and soon acquired a reputation for the eloquence of his words and for his ability to perform miracles.

Norbert was an early reformer of the Church—a precursor of St. Francis. His first attempts at reform failed. The members of the clergy found his ideas too austere for their liking. So Norbert decided to start fresh with thirteen disciples and founded his own order of monks. Because of their sincerity, poverty, and work among the common people, Norbert's order, known as the Premonstratensian, found support from the public. His monks came to represent a standard that other orders, like the Cistercians, began to emulate.

St. Norbert is the patron of Bohemia and the Premonstratensian Order that he founded. His feast day is June 6.

This card depicts the ability to have money and not be ruled by it and the ability to use money for creating beauty and well-being.

St. Lawrence • Knight of Coins

St. Lawrence stands holding a pot of coins and a gridiron, the symbol of his martyrdom. In the third century, St. Lawrence was the archdeacon of Rome under Pope Sixtus II and keeper of the treasury. During a time of persecution, the Emperor Valerian arrested the pope and all the other deacons and had them beheaded. One of the primary motivations for the emperor's edict against the Christians was the desire to confiscate the wealth of the Church. Lawrence was the only one of the Church hierarchy left, and as keeper of the treasury, he knew that his time would come soon. So Lawrence converted the property of the Church into money, and, combined with the money in the Church treasury, he distributed all of it to the poor and needy. Four days later when he was ordered to appear before the emperor with the treasures of the Church, he showed up with a multitude composed of the crippled, blind, and sick of Rome.

The emperor was not pleased, and thinking that Lawrence might have hidden the money, the emperor decided to have him killed slowly and painfully in the hope that he would reveal the hiding place. For the method of execution, the emperor chose to have Lawrence roasted alive on a gridiron. However, Lawrence never lost his composure, and as he was dying, he jokingly requested to be turned over because he was only half done.

St. Lawrence is the patron of comedians, deacons, the poor, librarians, cooks, brewers, confectioners, and restauranteurs, and he is called on for protection from fire. His feast day is August 10.

This card represents protection of financial and physical well-being and wise distribution of resources and investment. It can also represent someone we can count on and trust.

St. Elizabeth ▪ Queen of Coins

St. Elizabeth delivers coins to a poor youth. St. Elizabeth of Hungary was the daughter of King Andrew II. The princess was married to the landgrave Louis IV by arranged marriage. Elizabeth loved her husband and bore him three children. Wishing to share her happiness with the rest of the kingdom, Elizabeth dedicated herself to charity. She used her family money to found hospitals and orphanages and personally cared for the sick and needy.

In 1227, Louis participated in a crusade with Emperor Frederick II. While on the campaign, Louis died of the plague. At first Elizabeth did not want to believe that she was a widow. Eventually she resigned herself to the truth of her situation, but her troubles were just beginning. Her brother-in-law Henry made use of the situation to drive her from her home and stop her from dispensing the family money to the poor. Elizabeth refused to marry again; instead, she spent the remainder of her life as a Franciscan tertiary under the direction of the insensitive Conrad of Marburg. She devoted her life to poverty and work with the poor, the sick, and the elderly. She lived in such austerity and depravation that she became ill and died when she was only twenty-four.

St. Elizabeth is the patron of charities, bakers, beggars, the homeless, hospitals, and lacemakers. Her feast day is November 17.

This card represents prosperity, charity, and the ability of those in power to care for the less fortunate. Although St. Elizabeth ended her life in poverty, she never lost her joy and optimism. Her secret was that she always thought of others instead of herself.

St. Jude ▪ King of Coins

St. Jude Thaddaeus stands with a stick, the symbol of his martyrdom, displaying his coin with an image of Jesus on it. St. Jude Thaddaeus, the brother of James, was one of the Twelve Apostles, but there is little mention of him in the Gospels. Not much is known about him. He is believed to have been a healer and exorcist and to have preached in Mesopotamia and Persia with St. Simon. It is said that, along with Simon, Jude drove two devils out of a Persian temple. He was martyred by being clubbed to death.

Although Jude's full name is Judas, he is called Jude to distinguish him from Judas the traitor. St. Mark refers to him with the second name Thaddaeus ("strong-chested") to make the distinction clearer. However, the similarity was still great enough to cause his veneration to be neglected until the twentieth century. In modern times, his lack of veneration was noticed and it was assumed that of all the apostles, St. Jude would be willing to take on the lost causes that the others had neglected, reasoning that his own neglected state would make him sensitive to others' neglected needs.

As the patron of lost causes, St. Jude's popularity soared. Today he has become one of the most popular saints and is invoked more often than most. He is also the patron of hospitals, and is called on to find lost objects. His feast day October 28, which he shares with his friend and companion, St. Simon.

This card represents trust, total comfort with the physical world, and it can represent someone who can help in a time of need, especially if the situation seems hopeless.

ACE OF STAFFS

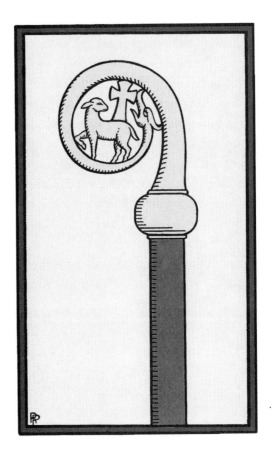

The head of a crosier, a bishop's staff, is carved with the *Agnus Dei,* the lamb of God, in the center of a serpent. The crosier is believed to be derived from the shepherd's crook or a walking stick; it signifies the bishop's role as shepherd of his diocese. The serpent represents the limits of the physical world and the lamb is Christ animating and sanctifying the world with his spirit. The suit of staffs is related to the element fire. This card represents the fire of life, the life force that is the soul animating the physical. It can mean a newfound passion or direction.

TWO OF STAFFS

Two staffs, one with the head of a serpent, the other with a vine, cross over a candle flame. This card represents opposites coming together with one passion.

THREE OF STAFFS

Three staffs cross, each carved with floral ornamentation. On the bottom, a ship approaches. This card tells us to expect reinforcements to arrive as needed, or else more of the same.

FOUR OF STAFFS

The marriage of Mary and Joseph is depicted with the Holy Spirit present. The four of the suit of fire is the physical manifestation of passion. This card represents commitment to our passions, a marriage, or a fertile situation.

FIVE OF STAFFS

Five staffs are related to five fingers. The hand displays the stigmata. Five is a significant number in all numerical systems because all peoples have used their fingers as a counting aid. The significance of the number five is given to us by the soul of the world through our hand. The stigmata signifies the spirit working through the hands. This card represents creativity and the ability to make our passions a reality through our hands.

Six of Staffs

This scene represents Christ's triumphant entry into Jerusalem. Jesus entered Jerusalem on the back of an ass and fulfilled the prophecy of the coming of the Messiah. The people rejoiced and laid garments and palms in his path. This card represents honors and victory, although the rejoicing may be temporary.

SEVEN OF STAFFS

Cain is shown killing Abel. Cain and Abel were the sons of Adam and Eve. Cain tilled the ground and offered the fruit of the field to God. Abel raised sheep and offered a lamb to God. God respected Abel's offering and not Cain's. In a jealous rage, Cain slew his brother. This card represents a power struggle, an argument, or violence.

EIGHT OF STAFFS

When St. Martin was offered the position of bishop of Tours, he refused it and hid. He had to be sought out and the position forced on him. This card represents cutting back on our passions, something that we may be in danger of overdoing. It can also represent a refusal or not living up to our potential.

Nine of Staffs

Under nine staffs stands a cross with two martyr's palms in front. This card represents sacrifice and martyrdom.

Ten of Staffs

Ten staffs interlock behind a phoenix rising from a fire. The phoenix is a symbol of resurrection. This card represents renewal, coming through an ordeal stronger for the experience. It may also refer to psychic energy that has been unblocked.

St. Roch ▪ Squire of Staffs

St. Roch stands with his pilgrim's staff displaying his sore. His faithful dog brings him bread. St. Roch was born in Montpellier, France, in 1295 to a rich family. When his parents died, he donated his money to the poor and went on a pilgrimage to Rome. On the way, he found himself in a plague-stricken area and took up residence as a hermit so that he could administer to the sick. He soon developed a reputation as a healer and had many miraculous cures to his credit. Eventually, however, he contracted the plague himself, represented in his icon by the sore on his knee. With little hope for survival, Roch retreated to a forest where he could not infect anyone and waited to die. Instead, a dog, who seemed to be his counterpart in the animal kingdom, miraculously found him and healed him by bringing him food and licking his wounds.

It is said that when Roch returned home after his illness, his appearance was so changed that his uncle refused to recognize him and had him imprisoned. While in prison, Roch was cared for by an angel, but after five years he died. After his death, his identity was confirmed when a cross-shaped birthmark was discovered on his chest. In an alternative account, Roch was falsely accused of spying in Angers, Lombardi, and died in prison there.

St. Roch is the patron of dogs, surgeons, knees, invalids, bachelors, the falsely accused, and offers protection from pestilence, cholera, plague, and other epidemics. His feast day is August 17.

This card represents adventure and setting out for a new area or enterprise. It also represents the humility it takes to admit our weaknesses and to accept help from others.

St. James ▪ Knight of Staffs

St. James stands with his Bible and his staff bearing his symbol, the cockleshell. St. James the Apostle is called the Greater to distinguish him from the other apostle named James who became a follower of Jesus later. St. James was a fisherman with his brother, St. John the Apostle. He was a follower of John the Baptist before coming to Jesus. James was witness to most of the miracles performed by Christ. After the Resurrection, he preached in Samaria, Judea, and some say Spain. James was the first apostle to be martyred. He was killed with a sword, which is sometimes depicted as another of his emblems.

According to legend, as James was being led to his death, the soldier who accompanied him was so overwhelmed by James's dignity and composure that he fell to his knees and confessed that he was secretly a Christian. James forgave him for not coming forward sooner with a kiss to the forehead and the words, "Peace be with you." The two were then martyred together. Because of this, the ritual of the Eucharist of the Peace is attributed to him. In this service, members of a congregation turn to one another and repeat James's last words.[1] It is traditionally believed that his body was entombed in Spain where it became a major destination for pilgrims (who adopted his shell as their emblem).

St. James the Greater is the patron of pilgrims, blacksmiths, knights, arthritis suffers, Spain, Chile, Guatemala, and Nicaragua. His feast day is July 25.

This card represents a pilgrimage, an adventure, or setting off to settle in a new destination. It can also represent the goal of our journey.

St. Genevieve • Queen of Staffs

St. Genevieve, the young shepherdess, stands with her crook and her lamb. Genevieve was a shepherdess born in Nanterre, France, in 422 who became a nun at the age of fifteen. When she was young, her mother went blind as a result of slapping her daughter in anger. Genevieve cured her with her tears. When her mother died, Genevieve became a nun and moved to Paris. In the Parisian nunnery, she became known for her mystic visions. In one trance, Genevieve prophesied disasters and invasions that would befall the city. Not accepting fate, she became determined to use her powers to protect the city. When Paris was besieged by the Franks under the command of Childeric, Genevieve headed a convoy along the river to bring food and supplies into the city. Later she used her courage and powers of persuasion to win Childeric's respect and gained the release of prisoners. She also foresaw the coming of Attila and the Huns, but through fasting and prayer Genevieve brought God's protection to the city and Attila changed direction before reaching Paris.

St. Genevieve's relics have continually been used to protect France from epidemics and disasters. The most famous cure attributed to her was during the ergo epidemic in 1129. Her shrine, however, was destroyed during the French Revolution.

St. Genevieve is the patron of Paris and is called on for protection from plague, fever, and disaster. Her feast day is January 3.

This card can represent both simple rustic passion, and great refinement and beauty. It also represents nurturing and protection.

St. Patrick ▪ King of Staffs

St. Patrick stands in bishop's dress on the shore of Ireland holding a crosier with his symbol, the shamrock, carved on its head. He points to the snake who leaves as he enters. St. Patrick was born in England in 387, but lived in France. As a young man, he was captured by pirates and sold as a slave in Ireland where he suffered for six years. One night he had a dream that told him he would escape and return home. Emboldened by the dream, he ran away and made his way over two hundred miles to the shore where he convinced some sailors to return him to France.

In France, Patrick entered the priesthood and advanced through study and effort until he was made bishop. Then he once again began having visions, but this time they told him to return to Ireland and spread the faith. With the permission of Pope Celestine, he did return as an evangelist, successfully converted the country in thirty-three years, and created a monastic community that became the greatest center of art and learning in western Europe in the early Middle Ages. It is said that Patrick converted King Laoghaire by demonstrating the mystery of the Trinity with a shamrock, and he is credited with driving the snakes out of Ireland.

St. Patrick is the patron of Ireland and is called on for protection from snakes. His feast day is March 17.

St. Patrick represents the power of the mind to let go of negative passions. The snake represents hatred, greed, fear, lust, and depression, and it departs when the mind is focused on love, compassion, and service to others.

CHAPTER 7

DIVINATION

Often the word *divination* is equated to fortunetelling, which means "to predict the future." Fortunetelling is often preached against by Catholics and other Christians for fear that it will lead one into breaking the first commandment. However, the Bible tells us of many devout prophets that were able to predict the future, and this is an ability that has been demonstrated by many saints as well. The problem that the Church has with fortunetelling is that it is not sure if all fortunetellers are receiving their messages from a divine messenger, and predicting the future can be fatalistic and unproductive.

Predicting the future is one of the least helpful things that one can do with the Tarot. A better use is true divination. The word *divination* literally means "to get in touch with the divine." It is derived from the Latin *divinus,* which meant "soothsayer," which in turn was derived from *deus,* meaning "God." We often think of the ancient soothsayers or oracles as making predictions. However, we have written records from Delphi and other oracles, and they show that the majority of statements of the oracles were not predictions but advice on how to make improvements and keep the favor of the divine.

When making decisions about relationships or careers, many of us have wished for a wise friend to turn to. With the Tarot, this source of wisdom can be found. It is inside us. We each have a higher, wiser self who can guide us toward our goals. In the center of our being, in our soul, we are connected with the soul of the world, Sophia, the divine wisdom of God. To contact wisdom we need to use our intuition, and the Tarot is a tool for intuition. Instead of predicting the future, the cards work best when they are used to help us create a more fulfilling future. We can use the Tarot for these ends and read the cards for others or for ourselves.

THE THREE-CARD SENTENCE

As we learned in chapter 1, the Tarot cards are hieroglyphs, a type of writing that uses pictures. These hieroglyphs can be used by our higher self to create sentences and communicate with the conscious mind. Therefore, the simplest and most powerful reading that we can do is the three-card reading. Once we have learned this technique, it can be used to build many different types of spreads to address different issues.

Three is considered a sacred number in most ancient cultures. In Christianity, it is related to the mystery of the Trinity. To the ancient Greeks, it represented the three points necessary to make the first geometric form and begin creation. Every complete sentence needs a subject and a predicate, but to go beyond the most rudimentary form of communication it will also need an object. Every story or situation has a beginning, middle, and an end. The Tarot trumps themselves are a three-part story. The three-card reading allows communication to happen.

To start, make sure that none of the cards in the deck are upside down in relation to the others. This will make it easier to place the cards right-side up in your reading. Right-side up cards allow the pictures to communicate more clearly and are less likely to throw unnecessary negativity into a reading. Some people feel that it is necessary to use upside-down cards to increase the vocabulary of the

Tarot and to allow for more possibilities, but this only doubles the possibilities. When we use three cards, we find that we have 456,456 possible combinations. If we use three cards for each position in a more complex reading, we have 456,456 possible combinations for the first place, 405,150 for the second, and 357,840 for the third place. With one card for each place with upside-down possibilities we have 156 possibilities for the first, 154 for the second, and 152 for the third. It is not necessary to confuse the reading with upside-down images.

Next, the querent must decide the purpose of the reading. The purpose can be a clarification of a past or present situation, to attain wisdom or advice, to investigate the possible outcome of a course of action, or to gain perspective.

Let the querent cut the cards once with his or her left hand (symbolizing the unconscious) while stating the purpose of the reading—it should be specific. Then you, the reader, should take the cards and shuffle them loosely and stop when you feel the intuition cease, or else let the querent shuffle them until the process comes to a natural state of completion. Let the querent cut the cards—again, with the left hand—by removing a block of cards from the top of the deck and setting it aside. Lay the first three cards from the remaining portion of the cut deck out in a line from left to right.

Now look at the cards as one picture. Look at the flow of energy in the picture, and interpret it as you would a dream or a story in a picture book. It is essential to notice in what direction the characters are facing. There are six basic patterns that can come up, although each has subdivisions, and at times two patterns can merge. The center card is most important to the action. The characters on each card can be facing left, right, center, or upward. At times the body is in one direction but a head or gesture points to the other or the figure may be pointing to both sides. It is usually possible to state the action as one sentence or expand it into a more detailed story. The six patterns are:

1. **Linear:** The cards could show a story that begins on the left and ends on the right, or the action could start on the right and proceed to the left. The figures will tend to be facing in the same direction, left or right. The end card may be facing forward or the opposite way to meet the action.

2. **Rejection:** Two figures may be back-to-back, indicating that the central figure is moving away from one side and all that that symbolizes and toward the other.

3. **The Central Origin:** Perhaps the central figure is looking directly at you with the cards on either side facing away from it. This may indicate that the action starts in the center and moves out to both sides, or if only one of the side cards faces away, to one side and not the other.

4. **The Central Destination:** When the end figures are facing the middle, the action may start on both sides and converge in the center. The center may be looking at you or its direction may be upward to a higher plain.

5. **The Central Problem:** The central card may also block the action or disperse the energy. The eight of swords may represent a block, the seven of swords may represent dispersion.

6. **The Central Teacher:** The central figure may be instructional and point to two possibilities illustrated by the cards that flank it.

Sometimes the layout may be interpreted as fitting more than one pattern. Use your intuition to determine which interpretation feels right. If you are confused by a card, you may expand it for clarification. This involves shuffling and obtaining another three cards for an expanded message related to the card in question. It is best to place these three above the card that they refer to. To find out the causes of a situation we may also place three cards below any card we need to know more about.

It is possible to use the three-card sentence for each position in many different spreads. You can also make up spreads of your own. The following is an example of a spread that I have used.

THE RELATIONSHIP SPREAD

Most questions querents have are about themselves in relationship to someone or something else. The relationship spread can be used for almost any question. It can be applied to relationships between two persons, or between a person and a job, home, culture, city, or other environment. It can be a health reading showing the relationship between the querent's mind and body.

The cards are laid out left to right in three groups of three. Start by letting the querent shuffle and cut as before. On the left, lay out the first line of three cards. These represent the querent. Skip a space, and on the right lay out the second line of three cards. These represent the other party in the relationship—person, place, job, and so on. If you feel that the three cards representing the other party belong to the left of the querent instead of the right, then follow your intuition. On top, bridging the gap between the two sides, place a third line of three cards. Lay the first over the last card of the group on the left, the second over the gap, and the third over the first card on the right. This will represent the relationship itself, and reveals the dynamics at work. Use the story approach to read each line of three as one picture. Then look at all three lines to see the bigger picture. It is helpful to notice how each side's group of cards change as they approach each other from the outside into the center. Always end with three additional cards of advice.

THE PERSONALITY CROSS

This spread was inspired by a dream of mine. It is based on the Jungian four functions of consciousness described in chapter 5: intuition, thinking, sensation, and feeling. It will be helpful to reread that section first, and to become more adept at this it will be necessary to read more about Jungian typology. Draw an equal-armed cross on a piece of paper and lay it on the table. Have the querent shuffle as before and lay out three cards at the each of four ends of the cross.

These cards will describe how the querent makes use of his or her talents to deal with everyday challenges and will help the querent understand how he or she is interacting with others.

Top: The cards at the top describe the person's dominant function. This is the function that the querent has been strong in since birth and that he or she relies on the most. The querent will tend to exhibit the most skill in this area and use this function consciously.

Bottom: This is the inferior function, the one in which the querent has been the most undeveloped in since birth. The more mature the personality, the more development will be seen here in the present. In most people it will still be undeveloped, and when this function is called for it may manifest in an immature or childish way. For example, the cards might indicate impatience, oversensitivity, or inappropriate reactions. In addition, because the conscious mind may be weak here, the unconscious will tend to be expressed through this function. The dominant function may represent the persona, and the shadow or the anima may be expressed in the inferior function position. The inferior function will always be on the same pole with the dominant. If the dominant is a rational function, like thinking, then the inferior will be the opposite rational function, feeling. If the dominant is an irrational function, then the inferior will be the opposite irrational function.

Left and right: The groups to the left and right represent the auxiliary functions. If the vertical pole was rational, then these will be irrational, and if the vertical pole was irrational, then these will be rational. As one matures, one or both of the auxiliary functions may be developed—usually before the inferior function is developed. Again, if one is not developed, it is a window for the unconscious. A masculine and feminine polarity may be apparent in these poles. In addition, as an individual matures, he or she may let a dominant function become weak or blocked in order to force a weaker function to develop. This tends to be a temporary situation.

After mapping out the querent's personality, we can ask the higher self to become involved. We can use an additional set of three cards to illustrate a possible bridge from one function to another. If we see a problem area, we may have the querent ask the higher self for a pattern in that area that will improve the situation. Then shuffle, cut, and replace the problem cards with three others. Again, always end with three cards of advice.

MEDITATION

Hieroglyphs or memory images were used for meditation, and this is something that we can do with the Tarot also. Start by picking a card that you wish to contemplate. Find a room where you will not be disturbed, and in that room find a comfortable place where you can sit with your back straight and upright. This can be the floor—a firm pillow is helpful—or a chair that does not cause you to slouch.

At first, solely pay attention to your breath until you find yourself breathing deeply and rhythmically from your abdomen. In this relaxed state, take the card and place it in front of you in a way that makes it easy to gaze on it. Now simply look at it without attaching any thoughts to it. Thoughts will naturally arise, but let go of each one as they do, watch them drift away, and then return to looking at the card. Begin to hold the image of the card in your mind. Visualize the border of the card as a doorframe, and the image on the card as a painting on a door. Visualize a handle on the door, reach out and grasp the handle, open the door, and visualize yourself walking through the doorway.

Look around. If all you see is darkness, look into it and wait—be patient. Feel free to allow yourself to interact with whatever images arise. At times it will seem that the characters on the cards have come to life. If they have something to show you, pay attention and play along with them. They are like teachers from within your psyche. The vision will come to a natural conclusion. When you are done, you may want to write your experience down. Jung called visualizations like this "active imagination," and he believed them to be the most effective means for achieving psychic health.

The trumps are some of the best cards to use for this meditation. Because they are organized in a story about the quest for enlightenment, we can go through them consecutively and experience the story as an internal reality. This is called the Fool's Journey. To take this journey is like being initiated into one's inner mystery. It is best not to work on more than one in a day. Take your time and contemplate each lesson.

Notes

Chapter 1

1. de Gebelin, *Monde Primitif,* 8:365. Translation by Joan Herman.
2. Kaplan, *Tarot Classic,* 37.
3. The information on pages 2–7 on the life and theories of Court de Gebelin and de Mellet is derived from Decker, Depaulis, and Dummett, *A Wicked Pack of Cards,* 52–72.
4. *Microsoft® Encarta® Encyclopedia,* s. v. "paper."
5. Pennick, *Games of the Gods,* 31–36.
6. Kaplan, *The Encyclopedia of the Tarot,* 1:24–34.
7. The information on pages 10–11 on the history of printing is derived from Hind, *Introduction,* 79–89.
8. Dummett, *The Visconti-Sforza Tarot Cards,* 6.
9. Yates, *The Art of Memory,* 12.
10. Graves, *The Greek Myths,* 1:125–26.

Chapter 2

1. Leonard, *The Teachings of Iamblichus,* 61–66.
2. Guthrie and Fideler, *The Pythagorean Sourcebook and Library,* 274.
3. Ibid., 174.

CHAPTER 3

1. Guiley and Place, *The Alchemical Tarot,* 14.
2. Guthrie and Fideler, *The Pythagorean Sourcebook and Library,* 133.
3. Ibid., 300.
4. Ibid., 70.
5. O'Neill, *Tarot Symbolism,* 185–88.
6. Kaplan, *The Encyclopedia of the Tarot,* 1:28.
7. Kingsley, *Ancient Philosophy, Mystery, and Magic,* 13.
8. This interpretation of Empedocles' poem is based on the work of Peter Kingsley in *Ancient Philosophy, Mystery, and Magic.*
9. Mish, *Webster's Word Histories,* 88.
10. Eliade, *The Sacred and the Profane,* 33–34.

CHAPTER 4

1. Decker, "The Tarot," 16–25.
2. The information on pages 74–75 is derived from Haskins, *Mary Magdalen: Myth and Metaphor.*
2. Graves, *The Greek Myths,* 1:125–26.
3. Fideler, *Jesus Christ Sun of God,* 39–42.
4. Armstrong, *A History of God,* 67–68.
5. Ibid., 25.

CHAPTER 5

1. The information on pages 150–151 is based on Jung, *Personality Types.*

CHAPTER 6

1. Morgan, *Saints,* 53.

BIBLIOGRAPHY AND RECOMMENDED READING

Armstrong, Karen. *A History of God: The 4000-Year Quest of Judaism, Christianity, and Islam.* New York: Ballantine Books, 1993.

Barnstone, Willis. "The Thunder, Perfect Mind." In *The Other Bible.* San Francisco: Harper & Row Publishers, 1984.

Decker, Ronald O. "The Tarot: An Inquiry into Origins." *Gnosis,* no. 46 (Winter 1998): 16–25.

Decker, Ronald, Thierry Depaulis, and Michael Dummett. *A Wicked Pack of Cards: The Origins of the Occult Tarot.* New York: St. Martins Press, 1996.

De Botton, Alain. *The Essential Plato.* New York: Quality Paperback Book Club, 1999.

de Gebelin, Court. *Monde Primitif.* Vol. 8. Paris: de Gebelin, 1781.

De Sola Chervin, Ronda. *Quotable Saints.* Ann Arbor, Mich.: Servant Publications, 1992.

Demarest, Donald, and Coley Taylor. *The Dark Virgin: The Book of Our Lady of Guadalupe.* Freeport, Maine: Coley Taylor, Inc., 1956.

Dummett, Michael. *The Visconti-Sforza Tarot Cards*. New York: George Braziller Inc., 1986.

Dunn-Mascetti, Manuela. *Saints: The Chosen Few*. New York: Ballantine Books, 1994.

Eliade, Mircea. *The Sacred and the Profane: The Nature of Religion*. Trans. by Willard R. Trask. New York: Harper & Row Publishers, 1961.

Englebert, Omer. *The Lives of the Saints*. New York: Barnes & Noble, 1994.

Farmer, David Hugh. *The Oxford Dictionary of Saints*. Oxford: Oxford University Press, 1992.

Ferguson, George. *Signs and Symbols in Christian Art*. New York: Oxford University Press, 1961.

Fideler, David. *Jesus Christ Sun of God: Ancient Cosmology and Early Christian Symbolism*. Wheaton, Ill.: Quest Books, 1993.

Gordan, Anne. *A Book of Saints: True Stories of How They Touch Our Lives*. New York: Bantam Books, 1994.

Graves, Robert. *The Greek Myths*. Vol. 1. Rev. ed. Harmondsworth, England: Penguin Books Ltd., 1960.

———. *The Greek Myths*. Vol. 2. Baltimore, Md.: Penguin Books, Inc., 1955.

Guiley, Rosemary Ellen, and Robert M. Place. *The Alchemical Tarot*. London: Thorsons, 1995.

Guthrie, Kenith Sylvan, trans., and David Fideler, ed. *The Pythagorean Sourcebook and Library*. Grand Rapids, Mich.: Phanes Press, 1988.

Haskins, Susan. *Mary Magdalen: Myth and Metaphor*. New York: Harcourt Brace & Co., 1993.

Hind, Arthur M. *An Introduction to a History of Woodcut*. Vol. 1. New York: Dover, 1963.

Hornblower, Simon, and Antony Spawforth, eds. *The Oxford Classical Dictionary.* 3d ed. Oxford: Oxford University Press, 1996.

Jones, Alison. *The Wordsworth Dictionary of Saints.* Hertfordshire, England: Wordsworth Editions Ltd., 1992.

Jung, C. G. *Psychological Types.* Bollingen Series, no. 20. Princeton, N.J.: Princeton University Press, 1971.

Kaplan, Stuart R. *The Encyclopedia of the Tarot.* Vols. 1–2. New York: U.S. Games, Inc., 1978–1986.

———. *Tarot Classic.* Stamford, Conn.: U.S. Games Systems, Inc., 1972.

Kingsley, Peter. *Ancient Philosophy, Mystery, and Magic: Empedocles and Pythagorean Tradition.* Oxford: Clarendon Paperbacks, 1995.

Leonard, George. "The Teachings of Iamblichus: Between Eros and Anteros." *Lapis,* no. 13 (2001).

McBrien, Richard P., ed. *The HarperCollins Encyclopedia of Catholicism.* New York: HarperCollins, 1995.

Mish, Frederick C., ed. *Webster's Word Histories.* Springfield, Mass.: Merriam-Webster Inc. Publishers, 1989.

Moakley, Gertrude. *The Tarot Cards Painted by Bonifacio Bembo.* New York: The New York Public Library, 1966.

Morgan, Tom. *Saints: A Visual Almanac of the Virtuous, Pure, Praiseworthy, and Good.* San Francisco: Chronicle Books, 1994.

O'Neill, Robert. *Tarot Symbolism.* Lima, Ohio: Fairway Press, 1986.

Panati, Charles. *Sacred Origins of Profound Things.* New York: Penguin, 1996.

Pennick, Nigel. *Games of the Gods: The Origin of Board Games in Magic and Divination.* York Beach, Maine: Samuel Weiser, Inc., 1989.

Scott, Walter, ed. and trans. *Hermetica: The Ancient Greek and Latin Writings Which Contain Religious or Philosophic Teachings Ascribed to Hermes Trismegistus.* Vol. 1. Boston: Shambhala, 1985.

Sharp, Daryl. *Personality Types: Jung's Model of Typology.* Toronto: Inner City Books, 1987.

Taylor, Thomas, and Floyer Sydenham, trans. *The Works of Plato.* Vol. 1. Somerset, England: The Promethius Trust, 1995.

Thompson, Della, ed. *The Concise Oxford Dictionary of Current English.* 9th ed. Oxford: Clarendon Press, 1995.

van den Brock, Roelof, and Wouter J. Hanegraaff, eds. *Gnosis and Hermeticism: From Antiquity to Modern Times.* Albany, N.Y.: State University of New York Press, 1998.

Walsh, Michael, ed. *Butler's Lives of the Saints.* San Francisco: Harpers San Francisco, 1991.

Yates, Frances A. *The Art of Memory.* London: Pimlico, 1966.

Index